KNOWLEDGE AN
UNDERSTANDING OF S
FORCES
A GUIDE FOR TEACHERS

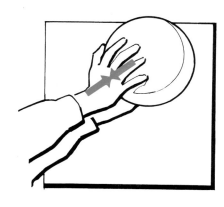
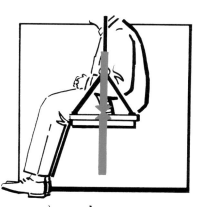

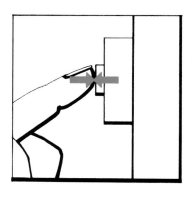

NCC
NATIONAL
CURRICULUM
COUNCIL

NCC is grateful to the staff at the Centre for Research in Primary Science and Technology, University of Liverpool, in particular Mike Schilling with the assistance of Hilary Atkinson, Eddie Boyes, Anne Qualter and Terry Russell, for their work in the development and writing of this book. Thanks are also due to David Malvern and Wynne Harlen, who acted as consultants; all those colleagues who offered feedback; and to the many LEA advisory staff, ASE officers, teachers and tutors in teacher training for their help in the preparation of this book.

£8 rrp
ISBN: 1 872676 64 2
Revised edition 1992
Copyright © 1992 National Curriculum Council

Printed in Great Britain

The National Curriculum Council is an exempt charity under the Charities Act 1960.

National Curriculum Council, Albion Wharf, 25 Skeldergate, York YO1 2XL

Chairman: David L Pascall

CONTENTS

INTRODUCTION

This book has been designed for teachers in primary schools. The book helps teachers to develop background scientific knowledge and understanding of forces. After working through the text and successfully completing the assessments, teachers will have covered those aspects of forces described in the programmes of study for Key Stages 1 and 2 of the National Curriculum science Order. The purpose of the material is to extend teacher knowledge and understanding; it is not suitable for direct use in the classroom.

How can the book be used?

The exercises can all be completed by one person working alone but clearly the work will be more stimulating if done with a group of teachers. No special scientific equipment is required for the practical tasks.

The book is intended to be used for:

* individual study;
* school-based staff development;
* INSET courses;
* initial teacher education.

Teachers needing to refresh their understanding can move quickly through the book by reading the 'What the scientists say' and 'Further thoughts' blocks of text found at the end of each section. Teachers who wish to deepen their knowledge and understanding can work systematically through the sections; this will take about 15 hours.

The content of the material

The book consists of nine sections, each of which could be a single study session. The structure of each section is as follows.

Tasks

These require teachers to think about a situation or carry out a practical task. They are printed on a yellow background.

Discussions

These help teachers to understand a particular idea used in completing a task. They are printed on a yellow background.

What the scientists say

When a key concept has been covered some text is included to give a summary of the idea from a scientific viewpoint. This text is printed on a green background.

Further thoughts

At the end of each section there is further information and descriptions of situations which allow teachers to think more about the science covered.

Concepts

A list of the concepts covered is given at the end of each section.

There are two levels in this book. The nine sections cover the aspects of forces described in the National Curriculum as follows:

Sections 1–6 cover levels 1–5;

Sections 7–9 cover levels 6 and 7.

Self-assessment

The reader is involved in self-assessment throughout the book as their own ideas are considered against those given in the text. At key points there are self-assessment sections which provide exercises on forces and also give feedback through the explanations in the commentary sections. Answers to questions are provided and a checklist of main concepts is given.

Resources

To help with the planning there is a resource section at the end of the book which lists the equipment needed to carry out the tasks in each section.

SECTION 1: FINDING OUT ABOUT FORCES

Thinking about forces

Forces cannot be seen and sometimes cannot be felt, though we may be aware of their effects, such as the forces which propel a boat or those which keep a shelf fixed to a wall. It is therefore natural not to think about forces at all.

There are many everyday meanings for the word *force*. What does it mean to you?

Task 1a

Write down your ideas – describing what a force *does* and defining what a force *is*.

Task 1b

Read the following three children's statements. Compare them with what you wrote for Task 1a.

(i) 'Force exerts pressure and pressure can push things. When I press something, it may move because of the pressure, or it may break.'

(ii) 'Force is the power to do something, to lift something or move it or hit it.'

(iii) 'Force is created by push and pull. If you move something, like a ball, it keeps going until it runs out of force.'

WHAT THE SCIENTISTS SAY: 1

How does a scientist use the word *force?*

Scientists describe a force as a *push* or a *pull*. Pushes and pulls can make things begin to move. Forces can cause moving things to speed up, slow down, stop, or change their direction. Forces can also make things change their shape.

None of the everyday words like *energy, power* or *pressure* is what scientists would accept as the definition of a force: they use such technical words in a special way. There are scientific definitions for pressure, energy and power. Although all these terms are related to force, none of them is the same thing as force (for definitions see the Glossary).

Discussion of Tasks 1a and 1b

You may have used the word *pressure*, as in statement (i) in Task 1b. Pressure is related to force. The same amount of force can exert different pressure, depending on the size of the area of contact. For instance, wearing snow shoes reduces pressure by spreading your force (weight) over a larger area and thereby reducing your force on the snow at any point.

The word *power* has been used in statement (ii) in Task 1b. For the scientist *power* is not the same as *force*. A force is quite simply a push or a pull.

Statement (iii) is very common in suggesting that a force is carried by an object. The *push* (or the *pull*) is the force. For example, a kick is the force to start the ball moving; the force does not keep it moving.

Where's the force?

Task 1c

Study each of these pictures and make notes to explain in your own words whether you think there are forces (pushes and pulls) in any of these situations and, if so, what the forces are doing.

(1) Lifting a bottle.

(2) Dropping a ball.

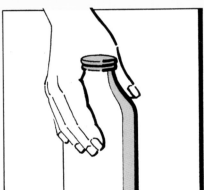

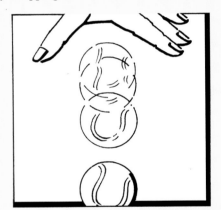

(3) Catching a ball.

(4) A book lying flat on a table.

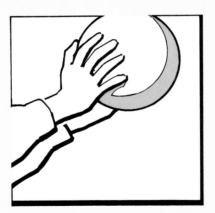

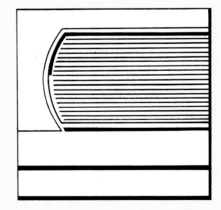

Drawing forces

Arrows can be used to represent forces. The *direction* of the arrow shows the *direction* of the force, the *length* of the arrow indicates the *strength* of that force.

The adult can push with a greater force.

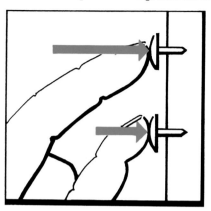

Task 1d

Sketch pictures (1)-(4) and draw arrows to represent the forces.

Discussion of Tasks 1c and 1d

Compare your notes from Task 1c and the drawings made in Task 1d with these explanations. Please note that for the sake of simplicity not all the forces acting on the objects are shown.

(1)   The upward force, exerted by the person pulling the bottle, is greater than the force down (the pull of gravity) so the milk bottle starts to move upwards.

(2)   The downward force (the pull of gravity) causes the ball to increase its speed towards the ground.

(3)   The force on the ball is the push by the goalkeeper's hand which opposes the ball's movement and causes it to slow down and stop.

(4)   There is a downward force (the pull of gravity) on the book. The reason for this is considered further in Section 3. The book exerts a push down on the table and the table pushes up on the book. These forces on the book are equal and cancel one another out. The book does not begin to move.

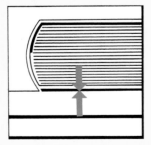

WHAT THE SCIENTISTS SAY: 2

What does a scientist say about forces acting in pairs?

When an object is stationary on the ground, there are two forces acting on it: the downward force of gravity and the force upward from the ground. The force of gravity causes the object to push down on the ground. As a result, the ground pushes back. This upward force is called the *reaction force* and it results from the push of the object on the ground. Whenever one object pushes another, the second object pushes against the first.

The concept of a *reaction* force is important in science and is summarised: EVERY ACTION HAS AN EQUAL AND OPPOSITE REACTION. (This is the third of Newton's three laws describing forces and movement.)

Task 1e

Sketch pictures (1)-(4). Using arrows to represent the direction and size of forces, describe the forces acting in each of these situations.

(1) A swimmer pushing against the wall of the baths to get a start for the next length.

(2) A ball rolling into a wall and about to rebound.

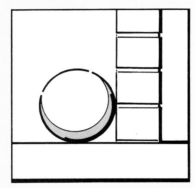

(3) Pushing a doorbell with your finger.

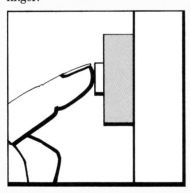

(4) Kneading dough.

Discussion of Task 1e

Compare your notes and drawings with these explanations.

(1) The swimmer is pushing against the wall; the wall pushes back and the swimmer begins to move in the opposite direction to that of his/her push. It is not that the wall supplies the *energy* (the swimmer does that) but it does supply the *force*, in *reaction* to the swimmer pushing on it.

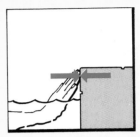

(2) At the moment it hits the wall, the ball is applying a pushing force to the wall. The wall pushes back on the ball with a *reaction force*, which causes the ball to change its direction of movement; it makes the ball rebound and roll away.

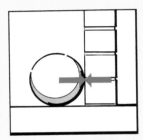

(3) The push on the doorbell makes it move as the spring is compressed. The button pushes back on the finger in reaction.

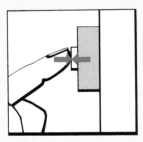

(4) The dough is pushed from above by the hands and from below by the table. The dough is squeezed out of shape.

Task 1f

In the following pictures the person pushes in the same direction. Make notes and drawings to show the direction of movement of the car and to explain how this happens.

Discussion of Task 1f

Compare your notes and drawings with these explanations.

In the first picture, the push is directly against the car and the car moves forward in the direction of the force. In the second case, the person pushes against the wall. The wall pushes back on the person in contact with the car. This causes the car to move backwards.

FURTHER THOUGHTS

Forces always appear in pairs

When an object is not moving, for example on the ground or on a table, you might imagine that there are no forces acting on it. On the Earth, however, the force of gravity is always present (see Section 3). If this force is always present, why do things stop moving downwards and rest on the ground? You might say that the ground is in the way. The ground is pushing back with an upward force called the reaction force.

Imagine that you are wearing a pair of roller skates. If you were facing a wall and pushed against it, you would begin to move away from the wall, backwards. It is as if the wall pushes you. Whenever you push against something, it pushes back at you. In this case, the wall would be pushing you as a consequence of you pushing the wall.

CONCEPTS

Forces are pushes and pulls.
Forces act in pairs.

SECTION 2: WHAT DO FORCES DO?

In this section we consider the effects that forces can have.

Task 2a

Look back to Task 1c. What are the forces doing to the bottle, the tennis ball, the football and the book? Describe the effect the forces are having in each case.

Discussion of Task 2a

The key words for describing these situations are found in 'What the scientists say: 1'. The milk bottle was at rest; the pulling force makes it *begin to move*. The falling tennis ball is made to *move faster* towards the ground by the force of gravity. The football *slows down* and *stops* as a result of the force of the catch. The book is *kept still* by the balanced forces of gravity and the push of the table.

Moving on the ground

Task 2b

What are the forces acting on these stationary trolleys? Explain any differences between the two situations by making notes and drawings.

Discussion of Task 2b

The same downward force pulls each of the trolleys (the force of gravity). The full trolley is *heavier* (in other words it pushes harder on the ground) because it has more things in it. The pushing force upward, from the ground, is greater on the full trolley. Both trolleys remain still because the downward force is the same as the upward force in each case, so the forces on each trolley cancel each other out.

Task 2c

Imagine pushing these two trolleys around a supermarket. You would need to turn them round at the end of each aisle and to stop and start them each time you took something from the shelf. What differences would you notice in moving the two trolleys? Describe these differences in terms of the forces involved.

Discussion of Task 2c

You need to consider the forces required to make a trolley start to move, to make it stop and to make it change direction. Each of these forces will be greater on the full trolley than on the empty one. You might also consider the force required to keep the trolley moving, which is sometimes quite large. Resistance to movement (friction and air resistance) is considered in Section 8.

Task 2d

Consider in the light of what you have read about forces, the following children's responses to the question 'Do you think there are any forces on this marble which is rolling across the table?'

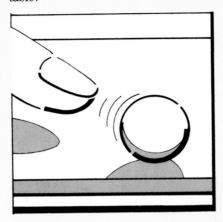

(i)   'Yes. The force which keeps it moving.'

(ii) 'The push.'

(iii) 'A rolling force. To keep it going round.'

(iv) 'No. No forces.'

(v)   'The pushing power.'

(vi) 'Friction.'

Make a note of your thoughts.

Discussion of Task 2d

Most of these children's responses illustrate aspects of a common idea that there must be a force *in* or *on* something which is moving that keeps it moving. This is not so. Response (v) includes the word *power* which scientists reserve for a more specific purpose (see the Glossary). Responses (ii) and (v) refer to the push. A push is a force and the push is no longer present so the force cannot still be acting on the marble. Response (vi) refers to friction which is considered in Section 8.

If moving objects do not carry force in them, what have they got which makes them different from when they are at rest? Responses (i) and (iii), for example, imply that the marble has something. That *something* is called momentum and is considered in Section 7.

WHAT THE SCIENTISTS SAY: 3

What does a scientist say about what forces can do?

Forces can act with other forces of different sizes and directions. A force can make something change its speed or direction; that is, it can make it *accelerate* . For example, a speed boat pulls a skier who starts to move. The skier has changed speed, or accelerated. If the boat then changes its speed **or** direction a scientist would say that the skier has accelerated. Notice that *accelerating* is used by the scientist differently from the sense in which we use it as drivers of cars. To travel at a steady 30km/h in a circle is, for a scientist, to be *accelerating* because of the change of *direction*.

Forces acting with other forces can make something accelerate. The greatest force contributes most, leaving what the scientist calls the resultant (or *net*) force. For example, in a tug-of-war the teams pull in opposite directions. The team which produces the greatest force wins, by making the other team change its direction of movement. The resultant force is that left over (i.e. not cancelled out) which makes the weaker team change direction. Forces can act together to leave no residual force. This would produce a draw in the tug-of-war.

Task 2e

Use the scientist's definition of *acceleration* to decide in which of the cases, described in Tasks 1c, 1d and 1e, objects were accelerating. Explain in each case how you came to describe whether or not acceleration was involved. Also, comment whether or not there are net forces in each case.

Discussion of Task 2e

The milk bottle accelerates upwards due to the net upward force.

The tennis ball accelerates downwards.

The ball is caused to decelerate and stop.

There is no net force on the book which is stationary on the table.

The swimmer accelerates away from the wall of the pool.

The ball accelerates away from the wall.

The bell push accelerates initially as the spring is compressed.

There is a resultant force on the dough causing it to change shape.

WHAT THE SCIENTISTS SAY: 4

What does a scientist say about moving objects?

There are three important *Laws of Motion* to explain the effects of forces. These laws were formulated about 300 years ago and are named after Sir Isaac Newton. Newton's First Law of Motion states that: 'An object continues in a state of rest or uniform motion in a straight line unless it is acted on by some external force.'

Moving in water

Task 2f

Think about what you know about forces to explain what is happening in each of these situations. Make notes and sketches and draw arrows to show the strength and direction of the forces which you describe.

(1)   A strong wind blows from behind, catching the sail, and causing the boat to move forward.

(2)   A strong current runs in the opposite direction to the boat's movement, slowing it down.

(3)   The engine is switched on to help the boat move forward against the current.

Discussion of Task 2f

(1) The forward force of the wind causes the boat to pick up speed – it accelerates in the direction of the force of the wind. There is some resistance to movement (a backward force on the boat) by the water. When the forward and backward forces are balanced the boat will not accelerate but will continue to move forward at a constant speed.

(2) The situation is as in (1), with the additional force applied to the boat (from the current) being in the opposite direction to the motion of the boat. This causes the boat to change its speed; it slows down.

(3) The propeller (driven by the engine) applies a force on the water and the water pushes back on the propeller. This increased forward force makes the boat accelerate. After speeding up, the forward force is matched by the backward resisting force, from the water. When these two forces are equal and opposite and there is no net force, the boat continues to move forwards at a steady speed.

Moving in the air

Task 2g

Screw up a piece of paper. Throw it in the bin. What are the forces on the paper at each of the stages shown in these pictures?

(1) Being thrown.

(2) In the air.

(3) In the bin.

Discussion of Task 2g

At each stage the force of gravity is pulling the paper. This is discussed in Section 3.

(1) The force from your hand on the paper pushes it through the air.

(2) Gravity pulls the paper down; there is also air resistance, slowing the paper down. This is discussed in Section 8.

(3) This can be compared with the book resting on the table in Task 1c. The paper exerts a push down equal to the push up of the bin. The paper does not move.

You know that the paper does not fly through the air for ever, just as a supermarket trolley would not run for ever if you pushed it and let it go. From Newton's First Law, it follows that there must be forces acting on the objects in each of these cases which cause them to slow down and stop. These forces are the forces of air resistance and friction and are considered further in Section 8.

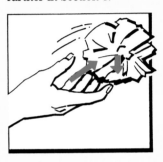  

FURTHER THOUGHTS

Speeding up and slowing down
If something is at rest it will remain at rest unless a force pushes it. If it is already moving, it may be difficult to imagine that it will carry on moving at a constant speed (for ever, according to the scientists) in a straight line unless some outside force pushes it either to make it go faster, to make it go slower or to change its direction of movement. Experience on Earth leads us to believe that nothing carries on moving for ever. The fact that on Earth things slow down and stop suggests that there are forces which cause this slowing down. These factors are described in Section 8.

What do forces feel like?
When a wind is very strong, you can feel it pushing against you. A loaded skip is heavy and is not moved by the force of the wind whereas small, light items of rubbish in it would be blown about. The same force can have a different effect on different objects. You are applying force when you open and close doors, pull the top from a pen, lever the lid off a can of paint, dig the garden or do any task which involves changes in movement or shape.

CONCEPTS

A force can make things start moving.
A force can make things move faster.
A force can make things slow down.
A force can make things stop moving.
A force can make things change direction.
A force can make things change shape.

SELF-ASSESSMENT: PART 1

Self-assessment is divided into four parts, each part is a continuation and extension of the sections that precede it. The last self-assessment section covers all the main ideas raised in this book. It is intended that you carry on learning about forces whilst working through the assessments.

Each self-assessment section contains several *Assessment Tasks*. These may require you to sift through the concepts about forces that you have learned and identify the most appropriate concept to apply to a particular situation; or it may require you to use a number of concepts and to put them together to solve the problem. You are not expected to be able to give the right answer to all the *Assessment Tasks* straight away. Use your notes to explore the problem and take time to think about it. Then write or draw your answer as fully as you can. Once you are satisfied that you have done as much as you can, look at the explanations which are offered in the *Commentary* section. Your words may be different but you might have used the same concepts and combined them in the same way. You might find that your answer is different. It may be because you have not fully grasped one of the concepts involved in the correct response. It may be that you need to revise certain concepts. The *Concepts Checklist* includes all the concepts which are covered in each section.

Once you have read the *Commentary* for each *Assessment Task*, read the *Answers* which follow the *Concepts checklist* and mark your own answers. When you have marked all the *Assessment Tasks* you can check up on which aspects you need to revise.

Before you work through this section, make sure you have covered the concepts in Sections 1 and 2.

Assessment Task 1a

Sketch the following pictures and draw arrows to represent the forces in these situations.

(1) A coin is pressed into a lump of modelling material, to make an imprint. What forces are acting on the modelling material?

(2) A waiter balances a tray on his hand. What forces are acting on his hand?

(3) A conker falls from a tree. What forces are acting on the conker?

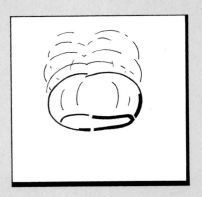

(4) A bag of nuts hangs by a thread from a tree.
  (a) What forces are acting on the bag?
  (b) Draw the forces again once the birds have eaten half the nuts.

Assessment Task 1b

The arrows indicate the strength and direction of the forces which are operating. Predict what you think will happen in each case, and explain why.

(1) A stationary toy on wheels is pulled.

(2) A house brick is placed on a flimsy paper bridge.

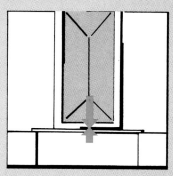

(3) A ping-pong ball, rolling towards goal posts, is blown at from one side through a straw.

(4) A plant in a pot is on a table. The soil is very dry. A lot of water is added to the soil from the watering can.

Assessment Task 1c

Look again at the four situations in Assessment Task 1a. Write predictions for what will happen in the following cases and explain your predictions. It might help to redraw and use arrows to represent the forces which are acting in each case.

(1) The modelling material is too cold and hard to be squashed.

(2) The waiter takes his hand away from under the tray.

(3) A strong wind blows sideways on the conker.

(4) The knot in the thread holding the bag to the tree comes undone.

Assessment Task 1d

Look again at the situations in Assessment Task 1b. Think about Newton's First and Third Laws of Motion. Look at your answers to Assessment Task 1b and identify where the First and Third Laws apply. Rewrite each answer referring specifically to these two laws.

COMMENTARY

Assessment Task 1a

(1) The pushing force on the coin also pushes down on the modelling material which in turn pushes down on the table. The downward force on the table causes an equal and opposite upward force on the modelling material. The modelling material does not push back on the coin with an equal force and therefore there is a net force acting down on the modelling material. This net force results in a change of shape (squashing).

(2) The force of gravity acting (downward) on the tray of glasses causes a downward push on the waiter's hand. The tray is not moving downward. There is an equal and opposite upward force, on the tray, from the hand.

(3) The force of gravity pulls the conker towards the ground with increasing speed.

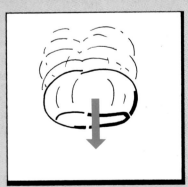

(4a) The force of gravity is pulling the nut bag down which means that it pulls on the string. But the bag is not moving. There are no net forces on the nut bag because the string pulls up with an equal and opposite force.

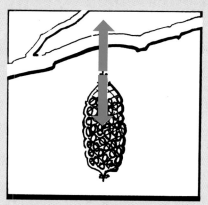

(4b) Once the birds have eaten half the nuts, the downward force on the bag of nuts is smaller (it weighs less); hence, as the bag does not move, the upward force of the string on the bag must be equal to the weight of the nuts and smaller than it was when the bag was full.

Assessment Task 1a continued

Assessment Task 1b

(1) The child pulls the toy. The pulling force causes the toy to begin to move (the toy accelerates).

(2) The force down on the bridge is opposed by a reaction force up on the brick. The forces on the brick are not balanced: the force **down** on the brick (due to gravity) is greater than the reaction force **up** from the bridge. The net force down on the brick causes it to start moving (to accelerate) down and the bridge breaks.

(3) The only force acting on the ball (ignoring friction and gravity) is the force of the blow This sideways force causes the ball to change direction (it accelerates) away from the goal.

(4) The downward force on the table is bigger when the pot is filled with water (it weighs more). The pot does not move therefore there is no net force on the pot. The upward force on the pot is equal (and opposite) to the downward force on the table.

Assessment Task 1c

(1) As with (1) in *Assessment Task 1a* the push down on the coin causes the modelling material to push down on the table. In this case the modelling material pushes back on the coin with an equal force, upward. It does not squash.

(2) Without the presence of the hand, the only force on the tray would be the downward force of gravity. The tray would be pulled down. This force would cause it to accelerate towards the ground.

(3) A strong wind would apply a sideways force to the conker causing it to change its direction of travel (to accelerate).

(4) When the knot comes undone, the downward force of gravity is the only force acting on the bag of nuts. This force causes the bag to accelerate towards the ground.

Assessment Task 1d

(1) The toy was at rest because there were balanced forces acting on it; there was a force *down* due to gravity and a force *up* from the ground *(Newton 3)*. The *pull* is the force causing a change in motion – acceleration forwards *(Newton 1)*.

(2) The net force down on the brick causes it to start moving (to accelerate) down and the bridge breaks *(Newton 1)*.

(3) There is no net horizontal force acting on the ball if we consider it to be moving at a steady speed in a straight line *(Newton 1)*. The blow down the straw is a force causing the ball to accelerate (change its direction of motion).

(4) The downward force by the pot on the table causes an equal and opposite force on the pot, upward, from the table *(Newton 3)*. There is no net force to cause the pot to begin to move *(Newton 1)*.

CONCEPTS CHECKLIST

The following concepts are covered in Sections 1 and 2.

Forces are pushes and pulls.

The *strength* of a force can be represented pictorially by the *length* of an arrow.

The *direction* of a force can be represented pictorially by the *direction* of an arrow.

Forces act in pairs.

Balanced forces mean there is no net force, therefore no change in motion or shape.

A force can make things change shape.

The force of gravity pulls things down towards the Earth.

A force can start things moving from rest.

A force can make moving things move faster, slower or stop moving.

A force can make moving things change direction.

Your explanation of Assessment Tasks 1a-1d should include the concepts listed above.

ANSWERS

Assessment Task 1a

(1) One arrow pushing down on the modelling material;
one pushing up.
There is a change of shape.

(2) Either: one arrow down and one arrow up of equal length;
or: one arrow down and five arrows up (one from each finger).
Length of down arrow equal to total length of up arrows.

(3) One arrow down.

(4) (a) One arrow pulling down; one pulling up.
Arrows of equal length.
(b) As for (a) but arrows shorter.

Assessment Task 1b

(1) The toy will move because of the pulling force.

(2) The paper bridge will bend and collapse because of the force of the brick.

(3) The ping-pong ball will change direction because of the force of the blow from the side.

(4) The pot will get heavier but not move because the table pushes back with an equal force.

Assessment Task 1c

(1) The modelling clay is not squashed because it pushes back with a force equal to the force down on the coin.

(2) The tray of glasses will fall to the ground because the downward force of gravity is not opposed by a force from the hand.

(3) The conker will change direction because of the force of the wind from the side.

(4) The bag will fall to the ground because the downward force of gravity is not opposed by any upward force from the thread.

Assessment Task 1d

(1) The toy will move because of the pulling force *(Newton 1)*. The force down due to gravity is opposed by an equal force upwards from the floor *(Newton 3)*.

(2) The paper bridge will bend and collapse because of the force of the brick *(Newton 1)*.

(3) The ping-pong ball will change direction because of the force of the blow from the side *(Newton 1)*.

(4) The pot will get heavier but not move because the table pushes back with an equal force *(Newton 3)*.

SECTION 3: GRAVITY

In Sections 1 and 2 you considered the forces which are present in everyday situations. The force of gravity was present in each case, but it was sometimes ignored, for example when the swimmer changed direction. Gravity could be ignored because the changes in movement were in a horizontal direction and gravity acts vertically.

WHAT THE SCIENTISTS SAY: 5

How does a scientist describe the force of attraction between two objects?

Newton's Law of Gravity says that EVERYTHING IN THE UNIVERSE ATTRACTS EVERYTHING ELSE. There is a force of attraction between any two objects, which depends on their mass and the distance between them. The force increases as the mass of the objects increases and as the distance between them decreases.

If you take any two objects — say a book and a pencil — they actually attract one another with an extremely weak force. The force is incredibly weak so you do not notice it. It is the force of gravity. If the two objects have more mass — say a car and a skyscraper — then the force between them is bigger. It is still very small but it is possible for scientists with very sensitive measuring apparatus to measure such forces. Because the Earth is the largest object of which we have experience, the only force of gravity we are aware of is that which the Earth exerts on us and the things around us.

Task 3a

(1) Can you think of any instances when something 'goes up' and does not come down again?

(2) Some children were asked: 'If you drop a potato and a fir cone of similar size from the same height, at the same time, what do you think will happen, and why?' Some teachers were asked the same question.

Their responses to the question are shown below. Summarise the children's ideas and those of the teachers.

What do you think will happen? Explain your prediction.

Children's ideas

(i) 'They'll both fall, the fir cone first because it's lighter, the potato second because it's heavier.'

(ii) 'They'll fall.'

(iii) 'They'll fall down, the potato first because it's heaviest.'

Teachers' ideas

(1) 'They will both fall to the ground because of gravity.'

(2) 'The potato will fall faster because it's heavier — heavier things fall faster.'

(3) 'If the cone is open it might be slower due to greater air resistance.'

Discussion of Task 3a

(1) A balloon filled with helium (which is a very light gas) does not come down until it bursts and the gas escapes. A rocket can push a satellite so far away from the Earth that the force of gravity is very weak. The satellite might never return to Earth.

(2) The children and teachers introduced 'heaviness' as a factor which might affect the rate of falling. Air resistance, which depends on the shape and size of the falling object, was introduced by one of the teachers. This is considered further in Section 8.

(3) Your prediction might be 'the potato will land first' or 'the fir cone will land first' or 'there will be no difference'. Your explanation of any of these predictions is a hypothesis. The hypothesis may be tested.

Task 3b

You need a potato and a fir cone of similar size. Note how you determined that they were of 'similar size'. Predict what will happen when they are dropped simultaneously. Test your prediction by dropping them from a reasonable height (e.g. standing on a chair). Record your results and note your conclusion.

Discussion of Task 3b

Did your investigation confirm your prediction?
Does the outcome support your hypothesis?
Were there any differences in how they fell?
How could you improve your investigation?
When you chose a potato which was the same 'size' as the fir cone did you interpret size as weight, shape or volume?

WHAT THE SCIENTISTS SAY: 6

What does a scientist say about gravity?

Gravity is the name of the phenomenon whereby two objects attract one another. The Earth has a large mass so the force of attraction is big and this force pulls objects to the Earth. The force is called the 'weight' of the object.

When objects have a very large mass (they are made up of a considerable amount of matter) — such as the Earth, the Moon, the stars and the galaxies — forces of attraction can become enormous. The force between the Earth and you — the force of gravity — is of particular interest. The force of attraction between you and the Earth holds you down and gives you your weight. You are pulled onto the Earth; this gives you the concept of 'down' as opposed to 'up'. That is why people on the North Pole, the South Pole and the Equator all consider down to be in the direction of the centre of the Earth.

Dropping things on Earth

Task 3c

You need a ball of modelling material and a large bag full of cotton wool.

(1) Make several balls of different sizes. Predict the order in which they will hit the ground if you drop them together.

Test your predictions.

(2) Now make a ball which has the same weight as the bag of cotton wool. Which one will fall to the ground fastest? Test your prediction.

Record all your predictions and results.

Discussion of Task 3c

(1) You were probably unable to detect any differences in the order in which the balls hit the ground. You might have predicted that the biggest (heaviest) ball would hit the ground first because the force of attraction is bigger. However, heavier objects need a bigger force than lighter objects to make them change speed and the forces (i.e. the force of attraction and the force needed to change the speed) cancel each other out (see Section 4). Light objects fall to Earth at the same rate as heavy objects when air resistance is the same.

(2) If you were able to drop the objects over a long distance (for example from a first floor landing) you will have noticed that the bag took a longer time to fall to the ground than the ball with the same weight.

This is an important discovery because Newton's Law of Gravity says that the force of attraction increases with mass. Things which are light for their size – or things which are not streamlined – drop more slowly. The reason for this difference is the force which acts to slow such objects down – air resistance. Air resistance slows down the bag of cotton wool. Without air, every object would fall at the same rate.

Dropping things on the Moon

Task 3d

Imagine repeating the experiments in Task 3c, on the Moon. Predict and record what you think would happen and explain your thinking.

Discussion of Task 3d

There is no air on the Moon, so there is no push up on objects which fall. Everything falls to the Moon's surface at the same rate. The falling is slower on the Moon than on the Earth. The mass of the Moon is less than the mass of the Earth, therefore the pulling force (gravity) on an object is less than that on Earth. The Moon pulls down on objects with one sixth of the force.

WHAT THE SCIENTISTS SAY: 7

How does a scientist explain what happens when objects fall on Earth?

The force of gravity is always present on Earth. That means that there is always a downward force pulling on an object. This downward force pulls on an object to start it moving and on moving objects to speed up their movement. The force of gravity is not the same for all objects. It is bigger for objects which have more mass. Objects with a bigger mass need a bigger force to make them begin to fall. All objects begin to fall (accelerate) at the same rate.

On Earth, some objects speed up faster than others as they fall. This is because there is a pushing force, upwards, on all falling objects, caused by the air. Once an object is moving, if the air resistance (resistance to movement) is the same size as the force of gravity the object falls at a constant rate. This upward push (air resistance) is considered further in Section 8.

FURTHER THOUGHTS

Forces of attraction
Everything and everybody experiences a pulling force towards the Earth. This force is the force of attraction which we know as gravity.

CONCEPTS

The force of gravity is the force of attraction between any two objects.
The greater the mass of an object, the greater the force of attraction.
Objects fall to Earth because of the force of attraction between the object and the Earth.
The rate at which all objects fall towards the ground is the same in a vacuum.

SECTION 4: MASS AND WEIGHT

Task 4a

Note what you think mass is and how, if at all, it is different from weight. Read the following statements made in everyday contexts and rewrite them if you think you can use the word *mass* instead of *weight* to make them scientifically correct.

(1) I have put on a lot of weight over Christmas – I must go on a diet so I weigh less.

(2) What weight of coffee do I get in a large jar?

(3) I cannot take this sack of potatoes – 25kg is too much weight for me to lift.

Discussion of Task 4a

Mass could have been used in each of the statements. You could say 'I put on more mass and as a consequence I have more weight'. It is not scientifically correct to say 'My weight is 60kg', because kg measures mass. The weight and the mass of the coffee can be measured. The *mass* of the coffee in a large jar is 250g, but that is not its *weight*. Similarly, 25kg describes the *mass* of a sack of potatoes, not its weight. The weight of the coffee and of the potatoes would be different on the Moon – although they would each still have the same mass.

WHAT THE SCIENTISTS SAY: 8

What does a scientist say about mass and weight?

Mass is often said to be 'the quantity of matter in an object'. The mass of an object is constant. A large mass of 1000kg (this is 1 tonne — about the mass of a car) would weigh a great deal on Earth and be heavy. Transported to the Moon it would still be a 1000kg mass because none of the matter in it would have been taken away. However, the weight would be about one sixth of its weight on Earth.

Mass is not really to do with how heavy an object feels, but how difficult it is to start it moving, speed it up, slow it down, stop it or change its direction (to accelerate it). The bigger the mass, the harder it is to make it accelerate. Imagine a 1000kg mass floating around in a spaceship. It might seem light, but it would still be difficult to push it to someone else.

Weight is defined as the force of gravity on an object. The Earth pulls you down and gives you your weight. The Moon is smaller than the Earth and has less mass, so when an object is on the Moon, it is pulled downwards with a smaller force than it would be on the Earth. This is why things are lighter on the Moon. They *weigh* less though their *mass* is the same.

Task 4b

Children made these statements about mass and weight. Is each of them correct? Why? Why not?

(i) 'Weight is a type of mass.'

(ii) 'Weight is a pull.'

(iii) 'Weight is not affected by gravity.'

(iv) 'An object has a mass whether or not there is gravity.'

(v) 'A falling mass has weight because of gravity.'

(vi) 'Weight is a force.'

(vii) 'An increase in gravity increases an object's mass and weight.'

Discussion of Task 4b

(i) No. The weight of an object is a measure of the force of gravity acting on it.

(ii) Yes. Weight is a measure of the Earth's pull.

(iii) No. Weight is different on the Earth and on the Moon, for example.

(iv) Yes.

(v) Any mass has weight, because of the pull of gravity.

(vi) Yes. On Earth it is the pulling force of the Earth's gravity.

(vii) No. A greater force of gravity gives an object greater *weight*, but does not change the amount of matter (mass) which it has.

Balancing scales

These indicate when the *mass* of the object on one side of the scales balances a known mass on the other side; mass is measured in g and kg.

A Newton meter

This is calibrated in Newtons to indicate the force down, which gives the object its *weight*.

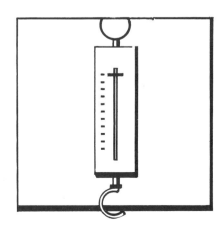

WHAT THE SCIENTISTS SAY: 9

What does a scientist say about weight?

The weight of an object can be measured by the pull of the Earth on it. Spring balances and other weighing devices are used to measure the force of gravity. Weight is a force and it is measured in NEWTONS. A Newton is defined as the amount of force which would make a mass of 1kg speed up by 1 metre per second, every second. A Newton is written as N.

In other words it is defined as how much it makes things speed up. In everyday language, people may say that an object has a weight of 3kg, but it is more correct to say that it has a mass of 3kg, and a weight (on Earth) of about 30N. On Earth 1kg weighs about 10N.

Weight = Mass × 10N (on Earth)

Task 4c

You will need: a bar of soap, a bag of sugar, a bottle of milk and a bag of potatoes.

Put the soap in your hand and 'feel' the weight.
Now put the 2kg bag of sugar in your hand. How big do you think the force pushing down on your hand is?
Pick up a milk bottle and put it on the table. What force was required to lift the bottle?
Try to pick up a 5kg bag of potatoes. What will you need to lift it?

Discussion of Task 4c

The force down (exerted by gravity) on 100g on your hand is about 1N and on the 2kg bag of sugar the force down on your hands is about 20N. To lift 5kg off the ground a force of at least 50N is needed. Scientists do not use g and kg to record the weight of objects; they use Newtons. What are commonly referred to as 'weights' should more accurately be called 'masses'.

Task 4d

You will need: an unopened pack of butter, a paper clip, an elastic band, balance scales (with two pans), masses, string and scissors.

The length, width and height of the pack of butter are three properties which do not change (unless you eat, squash or melt it); neither does the mass. Put the butter on the scales; balance the scales with some of the masses. You have measured the mass of the butter. You are used to calling this weight, but you know that scientists call it the mass, which is a measure of how massive the butter is (not how big, but how much 'stuff'). To determine the mass, you measure it using a balance.

Task 4e

Tie the string around the butter. Hook the paper clip around the string and the elastic band. Lift the elastic band until the butter is hanging in the air. What happened to the elastic band? Why do you think it has happened? Make a note of your ideas, using scientific terms.

Discussion of Tasks 4d and 4e

While you are pulling the elastic band upwards, the force of gravity is giving the butter weight by pulling it downwards. The weight of the butter is its 'heaviness'. Your pull up and the weight pulling down stretch the elastic band. The length to which the elastic band stretches indicates the strength of the force of gravity acting on the butter.

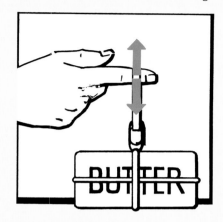

Task 4f

You will need a set of bathroom scales, an elastic band and ruler, or a Newton meter.

(1) Can you exert a push on the wall equal to the 'push' which you exert when standing on the bathroom scales? By leaning on the scales against the wall you can note the size of your push; record the size of this force.

(2) Find out how much pull it requires to open the fridge door, using the elastic band and the ruler, or the Newton meter. Record the size of this force.

Discussion of Task 4f

In Tasks 4c and 4d you were picking things up – exerting a pulling force in the opposite direction to that of gravity. In Task 4f you used horizontal pushes and pulls. You will need to convert your push, if it is registered in kg on the bathroom scales, into Newtons (remember the force on 1kg is about 10N, on Earth). For example, if you record 70kg when you stand on the scales, your weight is actually 700N.

Measuring forces, away from the Earth

Imagine a 1kg mass

on Earth   on the Moon   in space.

Task 4g

Estimate what would be the weight of the mass in each of these situations. Record the weights and your reasoning.

Discussion of Task 4g

On Earth the 1kg mass will weigh 10N.

On the Moon the force of gravity is one sixth as great as the force of gravity on the Earth (Newton's Law of Gravity) and the 1kg mass will weigh about 1.6N. This means that the weight of objects on the Moon is one sixth of their weight on Earth. In space, assuming that the mass is so far away from any planet (or any other mass) that there is no measurable force of gravity, it will be weightless, i.e. 0N.

Task 4h

Imagine that you have been transported to the Moon to repeat Tasks 4d and 4e. If you measured the length, width, height, mass and weight, which would be the same as on Earth? Which would be different? Why?

Discussion of Task 4h

On the Moon, the weight of the butter would be less and the elastic band would not stretch as much. The butter would be less heavy because the Moon is *less massive* than the Earth; the force of gravity is less. The butter would still contain the same amount of matter and so would have the same mass.

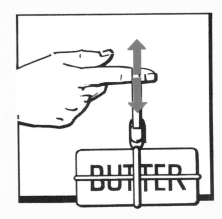

FURTHER THOUGHTS

Measuring forces

Force is measured in NEWTONS - by using a spring balance or scales. These measuring instruments actually measure the same thing – the force pulling an object down. This force depends on the mass of the object. Scales and balances can therefore be calibrated to measure *mass* **or** *weight* on the Earth.

You might find that the distinction between mass and weight is not made clear in some maths books. For example, exercises are sometimes set which require children to 'find the weight' or a set of objects and record their results in kg.

You feel forces when you lift things; you use more force to lift something which has more weight.

CONCEPTS

Mass is not the same as weight.
Mass is the amount of matter in an object.
Weight is a measure of the force of gravity on an object.
Mass is the quantity which determines the amount of force needed to begin to move an object.

SELF-ASSESSMENT: PART 2

Before you work through this section, make sure you have covered the concepts in Sections 3 and 4.

Assessment Task 2a

Which object do you think will hit the ground first in each situation? Explain why you think so?

(1)

(2)

(3)

Earth

Earth

Moon

(4) For each of the pictures (1), (2) and (3), list the variables which are controlled and those which change.

(5) In cases (1) and (2), will there be any difference in the speed with which the 1kg mass hits the ground? If there is a difference, why is this?

(6) In cases (2) and (3), will there be any difference in the speed with which the 1kg mass of lead hits the ground? If there is a difference, why is this?

Assessment Task 2b

Describe the forces here.

A small rock passes close to a huge asteroid in space.

Explain what you think will happen, and why.

Assessment Task 2c

Calculate the weight of the 12kg mass on each of the following.

Saturn   *Earth*   *Mars*

Gravity 1.1 times
that of the Earth   Gravity 0.4 times that
                                                         of the Earth

Assessment Task 2d

Sketch the following illustrations and draw arrows to scale to represent the forces on the object which is on a box in each case. Calculate the approximate forces, in Newtons.

(1)   (2)   (3)

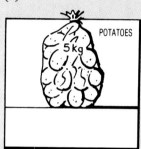   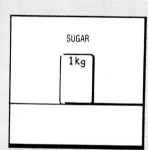   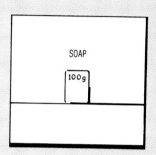

Assessment Task 2e

Copy the following illustrations and draw and explain the forces on the person in each case.

(1) 50kg person.   (2) 150kg person.   (3) 150kg person.

Earth   Earth   Moon

In cases (1) and (2) will there be any difference in the force required to start the person swinging? If there is a difference why is this?

In cases (2) and (3) will there be any difference in the force required to start the person swinging? If there is a difference, why is this?

Assessment Task 2f

Copy, draw and describe the forces acting on the 5kg mass.

(1)

(2)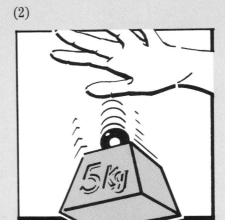

COMMENTARY

Assessment Task 2a

(1) The force down on the lead and the feathers is the same because they both have the same mass. There is a force up due to air resistance on both as they fall. Because the bag of feathers is huge the force up is relatively large so it is not streamlined. The force up on the lead is small, relative to the force of gravity. The effect of air resistance is therefore significant on the feathers and insignificant on the lead. The lead will hit the ground first.

(2) Lead is heavy for its size. The effect of air resistance (a force up) is negligible in both cases. They will hit the ground together, because the force of gravity makes them accelerate at the *same* rate.

(3) There is no air resistance on the Moon. The force down is the same on both objects because they have the same mass. Their acceleration is the same. They will hit the ground together.

(4) In (1) the heights are the same, the mass is the same but the materials are different.

In (2) the height and material is the same for each mass, but the mass is different.

In (3) the height is the same for each mass and the mass is the same, but the materials are different.

(5) The mass which travels further accelerates for a longer time. This means that (because the upward force is negligible) it hits the ground at a higher speed.

(6) The planet in (3) is different from that in (1) and (2) and the acceleration due to gravity on the Moon is one sixth that on the Earth. Both masses travel for the same distance but the force of gravity, which is less on the Moon, causes the mass on the Moon to pick up speed at a slower rate. It will hit the ground at a lower speed.

Assessment Task 2b

The force of attraction on the asteroid (due to the rock) and the force of attraction on the rock (due to the asteroid) are equal, and opposite (Newton's Third Law, applied to gravitational forces). However, because the rock only has a small mass it will move towards the asteroid. Both objects are moving in space. The force of attraction between them will alter their paths, each will be deflected. The rock, having less mass, will be deflected more than the asteroid.

Assessment Task 2c

Weight = Mass × 10N (on Earth).

The weight is proportional to the mass, so:

Weight (on planet X) = Mass × 10 × (relative size of the gravitational pull of the planet X).

Assessment Task 2d

(1)

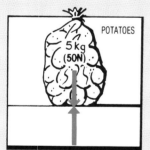

(2)

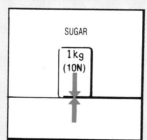

(3)

Weight = Mass × 10N (on Earth).

The forces on the object are gravity pulling down and the upward force by the box. The forces are equal and opposite.

They balance, so there is no net force on the object and therefore, in each case, no movement.

Assessment Task 2e

(1) 50kg person.

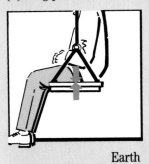

(2) 150kg person.

(3) 150kg person.

Earth

Earth

Moon

In each case the forces on the person are equal and opposite. This is similar to the book on the table (in Task 1c) and the objects on the box (in Assessment Task 2d). The gravitational force pulls each person down. The swing pushes up. This is a reaction force up, which is a consequence of the push down on the seat.

The pushing forces required in (2) will be greater than those in (1) because the mass is greater.

The pushing force required in (2) and (3) will be the same, because the mass which starts to move is the same in each case.

Assessment Task 2f

(1) A pulling force up, by the hand.

A pulling force down, by the Earth (its weight).

(2) There is a pulling force down on the mass due to gravity. There is a very much smaller force up due to the air resistance. This is discussed in Section 8.

CONCEPTS CHECKLIST

The following concepts were covered in Sections 3 and 4.

Mass is the amount of matter in an object.

Mass is the quantity which determines the amount of force needed to begin to move an object.

The force of gravity is the force of attraction between two masses.

The larger the masses, the larger the force of gravity between them.

The rate at which all objects fall towards the ground is the same.

Weight is a measure of the force of gravity on an object.

Your explanation of Assessment Tasks 2a-2f should include the concepts listed above.

ANSWERS

Assessment Task 2a

(1) The lead will land first. Air resistance slows the feathers down. Otherwise they would fall at the same rate.

(2) They will land together. Air resistance effect is negligible.

(3) They will land together. There is no air, so no upward force.

(4) In (1) height and mass are controlled; the materials are different.
In (2) height and materials are controlled; the mass is different.
In (3) height and mass are controlled; the materials are different.

(5) The one which travels further will hit the ground at a higher speed.

(6) The one on Earth has a greater acceleration.

Assessment Task 2b

The saucer and the rock are attracted to each other by the force of gravity.

Because the rock has a relatively small mass it will move towards the saucer at a much greater rate than the saucer will move.

Assessment Task 2c

Saturn:	Weight = 12kg × 10 × 1.1	= 132N
Earth:	Weight = 12kg × 10 × 1	= 120N
Mars:	Weight = 12kg × 10 × 0.4	= 48N

Assessment Task 2d

Two arrows are of equal length and point in opposite directions, in each case.

(1)   50N

(2)   20N

(3)   1N

Assessment Task 2e

In each case the force down (gravity) is equal to the force up.

More force will be needed to start to move the person with the most mass.

Assessment Task 2f

(1)   Balanced forces.

(2)   A force down.

SECTION 5: FLOATING AND SINKING

Why do things float?

Read the responses to the question which follows.

If a glass test tube, a small glass bottle and a large plastic bottle are put into a tank of water, what do you think will happen and why?

Children's ideas

(i)   'The heaviest will sink; the glass bottle.'

(ii) 'The heavy ones will sink.'

(iii) 'It'll float if we can trap some air in.'

Teachers' ideas

(1) 'With lids on they'll all float because they are full of air. Air is lighter than water.'

(2) 'If they are full of water the glass bottle will sink but the plastic one may still float because it is lighter.'

(3) 'They will fall on their sides and float, because they are full of air and water is heavier than air.'

Task 5a

(1) Summarise the children's ideas.
     Do you agree with the teachers' ideas?
     Rewrite the ideas to make them scientifically correct.
     Predict what you think will happen to each of the bottles and try it for yourself.

(2) Take a large empty plastic bottle (fabric conditioner or shampoo, for example) and screw the top on tightly; fill the sink or the bath with water and try to push the bottle under the water. What happens?
     Draw the forces which are acting on the bottle as it is held under water.
     Push the bottle to the bottom of the water. What happens when you let it go?
     Explain what you think is happening.
     Put the bottle: (a) on the floor and (b) on the water. Illustrate what is happening in terms of the forces which are acting on it in each case.

Discussion of Task 5a

(1) The children's ideas use the concepts that 'heaviness' causes something to sink and that 'air' is associated with floating. The teachers have the same ideas but the second teacher appears to recognise the significance of plastic being 'lighter' than water.

The bottles will float if they have lids on to trap air in them. The test tube will sink if it fills with water.

(2) There are two forces on the floating bottle – a push up from the water and the pull down of gravity. When you held the bottle under the water, you could feel the upward push of the water on the bottle. When you let go, the way in which the bottle shot up to the surface demonstrated the size of the force pushing it up. The net force on the bottle, when it was released by you, was upward.

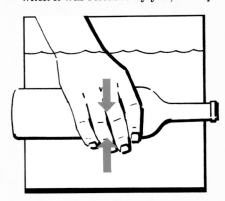

There is no difference in situations (a) and (b). The forces on the bottle are balanced. There is a pull down, due to gravity and a push up from either the floor or the water.

(a)   (b)

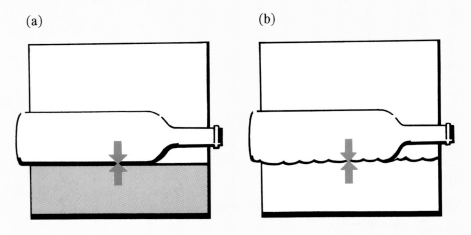

Task 5b

You will need a collection of objects (some of which do not float), some string, a paper clip, an elastic band and a ruler as used in Task 4d.

Suspend each object in turn from the elastic band to find a measure of its weight in the air by recording the length of the elastic band in each case. Next, lower each object into the water so that it is just below the surface and, again, record the lengths of the elastic band. Calculate the differences in length of the elastic bands when the objects are in and out of the water.

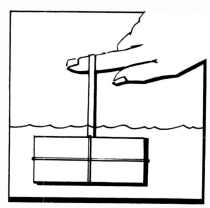

Discussion of Task 5b

The elastic band is always shorter when finding a measure of the weight of each object in water. The forces on an object which does not float and which hangs from the elastic band are: the pull up by the elastic band; the pull down by gravity; the push up by water. They are balanced. You can feel the size of the push up due to water by suspending the object in air and pushing up on the object with your finger from below with enough force to make the elastic band the same length as when the object is in water.

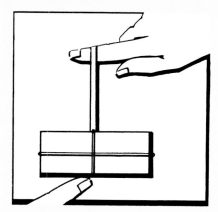

If the object floats the elastic band need not be pulled at all.

Task 5c

(1) Make a cup of tea by pouring water in the cup and slowly lowering the tea bag into the water. What do you notice about the water level?

(2) You need a ball of modelling material and a bowl of water. Make the modelling material into a boat shape. Draw the boat; predict whether you think it will float; test it and record your result. Now make another boat shape and repeat the experiment. Try this for a number of different shapes but always using all of the modelling material. Was the weight of each of your boats the same?

(3) Find the 'best' boat by adding ballast until the boat sinks. Use paper clips or marbles, for example, and increase the load until it sinks. What characterises the best of the boats? Draw the forces acting on a boat: (i) before adding the load; (ii) still floating with ballast; and (iii) when it sinks.

Discussion of Task 5c

(1) The level of water in the cup rose when you put the tea bag in. The rise in the level is due to the displacement of the water by the tea bag.

(2) Each of your boats was made from the same piece of modelling material; they were all made from the same mass of material so they were each of the same weight but they may not all have floated.

(3) As the volume of water displaced by the boat increased, so the push upwards by the water increased. When the boat floated, the force down (its weight) was equal to the push upwards. The addition of ballast to the boat increased the downward force, so the boat floated a little lower in the water, to displace more water and increase the push upwards. The best boats, which held the most ballast, displaced the most water.

WHAT THE SCIENTISTS SAY: 10

What does a scientist say about floating?

Archimedes' Principle says that the upward force (the upthrust) on an object floating in a liquid is equal to the *weight* of liquid displaced by the object. An object floating in water can be thought of as taking the place of the water. The volume of water which the object has displaced has a certain weight and that weight is the same as the force of the upthrust.

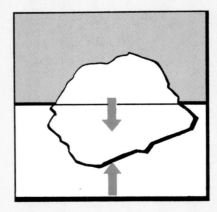

Task 5d

Imagine having two identical suitcases.

(1) Full of clothes.

(2) Full of books.

Which suitcase has the greater mass? Which has the greater weight?
Which has the greater density?

Discussion of Task 5d

Each of the suitcases has a different mass and each one therefore has a different weight. The suitcase full of books has a greater mass than the one with the clothes in. However, both suitcases are the same size; they have the same volume. The suitcase full of books is more densely packed than the other; it has a greater density. The density of an object is not only to do with its mass but how much space that mass takes up.

Most woods have a lower density than most metals. Most woods float because the forces balance, as shown in the diagram.

weight down

upthrust, from water

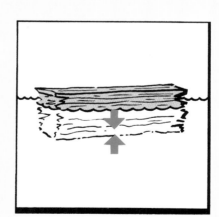

Density

Consider the density of a number of everyday materials.

Material	Volume (cm³)	Mass (g)	Weight (N)	Density (g/cm³)
Brick	260	652	6.52	2.5
Cheese	260	282	2.82	1.08
Wood	260	116	1.16	0.4
Butter	260	250	2.5	0.9
Expanded polystyrene	260	4	0.04	0.01
Soap	260	284	2.84	1.09

Task 5e

You need a collection of objects. Find their mass and their volume and calculate their density. Copy the table and add this information to it.

You will need kitchen scales to find the mass. The volume of objects which are difficult to measure, like an apple or a candle, can be measured by immersing them in a measuring jug of water. If the object floats push it down so that it is just below the surface of the water. Note the rise in the water level, this is the volume of the object.

Predict whether each of the objects will float and test your predictions.

Discussion of Task 5e

Your observations and the information given in the table will indicate that all objects with a density less than 1g/cm³ float. You can also see from the table that volume and mass are not the same, therefore large objects are not necessarily heavier than smaller objects made of different materials.

WHAT THE SCIENTISTS SAY: 11

What does a scientist say about the property of density?

The density of a material is the amount of matter in a given volume. The amount of matter is the mass of the object and is usually measured in grams (g). The volume is usually measured in cubic centimetres (cm³).

Density is defined as the MASS per UNIT VOLUME of a material and is usually measured in g/cm³.

$$DENSITY = \frac{MASS}{VOLUME}$$

Task 5f

You will need modelling material, table-tennis balls and scissors. Make your modelling material into a ball which is the same size as a table-tennis ball. Find the volume of a table-tennis ball by immersing it in a measuring jug of water (as in Task 5e). To change the density of the ball, make a hole in it with scissors, and fill it with water, modelling material or metal weights, or any other suitable material. You have increased the mass without changing the volume: you have increased the density.

(1) Measure the mass of the filled table-tennis ball and calculate its density. Test whether the filled ball floats.

(2) Change the density of the modelling material ball, keeping the mass the same, but changing its shape: make it into a 'coracle' shape. This will have the effect of changing the volume, as shown in the illustration below. The shape can be considered as being partly modelling material and partly air. The mass of this shape is made up of air and modelling material.

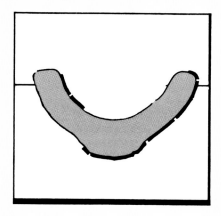

Discussion of Task 5f

You have been able to make a 'floater' sink and a 'sinker' float. Factors which affect floating and sinking in water include the shape and the density of the object.

Task 5g

You will need a 5cm³ teaspoon, salt or sugar, some scales and a waterproof container.

(1) Measure 25cm³ of water and weigh it. Calculate the density of the water.

(2) Slowly add as much salt (or sugar) as you can, stirring to dissolve it. When all the solid is dissolved, carefully measure the weight and the volume of the solution. Calculate the density of this solution.

Discussion of Task 5g

(1) Every cubic centimetre (cm^3) of water weighs 1g at room temperature. The density of pure water is $1g/cm^3$.

(2) The density of the salt solution is greater than $1g/cm^3$, so the upthrust of each cm^3 displaced will be greater. This explains why objects float better in the sea; the salt dissolved in sea water makes it more dense and it provides more upthrust than pure water.

FURTHER THOUGHTS

The push upwards from water

Archimedes' Principle suggests that if more water is displaced, the push upwards by the water on an object will be greater. It is possible to measure the push up from water by weighing objects in air and in water and then calculating their change in weight.

What makes things float or sink?

The shape of an object is important in deciding whether it floats or sinks. The material from which the object is made (whether it is waterproof) also determines whether it floats. Density is also important in floating and sinking. Changing density can change an object's ability to float.

Density of liquids

The upthrust on an object floating in water is equal to the *weight* of water the object displaces. If the density of the water is increased, the upthrust exerted by a certain volume will increase. The density of water can be increased by dissolving a solid in it. For example, salt dissolves in water. You probably know that you can float better in the sea than in a swimming pool. This is because of the salt dissolved in sea water and salt water is more dense than the water in the swimming baths.

CONCEPTS

Floating objects are pulled down by the force of gravity.
A push upwards from the water makes some objects float.
Factors which affect floating and sinking include the density and shape of an object and the density of the liquid.

SELF-ASSESSMENT: PART 3

Before you work through this section make sure you have covered the concepts in Section 5.

Assessment Task 3a

A water candle is floating in the glass bowl at the centre of the dinner table.

What do you think will happen to the floating candle as it burns?
What will it look like by the end of dinner?
Why do you think this is? Make notes to explain your answer.

Assessment Task 3b

Copy and complete this table.

Item	Volume (cm³)	Mass (g)	Density (g/cm³)	Floats or sinks
Sprout	25	20	0.8	
Tomato	40	60	1.5	
Potato	120	130	1.1	
Apple	210	160	0.8	
Banana	125	120	0.9	
Pear	130	140	1.1	
Orange	200	160	0.8	
Carrot	70	80	1.1	
Grape	6	7	1.2	

Describe why you think some things would float and others sink.

Assessment Task 3c

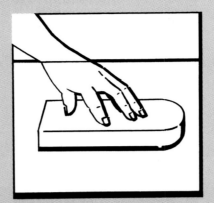

(1) A swimming float is held under water. Copy and draw the forces acting on it.

(2) What will happen to the float when you let go?
Explain the forces acting on the float when you've just let go.

(3) What would be different about the forces if the float was replaced by a piece of stone?

Assessment Task 3d

(1) Explain, in terms of the forces involved, why ice floats on water.

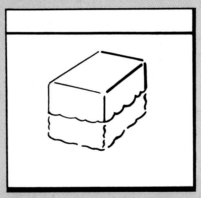

(2) Explain in terms of the forces involved, why a new plastic sponge floats on top of the
water and an old one floats just below the surface.

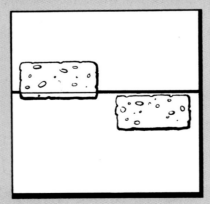

COMMENTARY

Assessment Task 3a

As the candle burns, the total mass decreases (wax burns away, it combines with oxygen and turns to gas) so the candle will float higher in the water (the opposite effect to adding ballast to the modelling material boats).

Assessment Task 3b

The push upwards on each of the fruit and vegetables which floats is equal to its weight. The weight of each of the items which sinks is greater than the push upwards. All the *floaters* have a density of less than $1g/cm^3$. Objects which float in water have an average density which is less than $1g/cm^3$.

Assessment Task 3c

(1) When the float is held under water it is not moving. The forces on the float are balanced. There is a push down (from you), a pull down (from the Earth); there is a push up (from the water).

(2) At the moment you let go, the net force is up – so the float moves to the surface of the water. Floating on the surface, very little water is displaced to balance the pull down (the weight of the float).

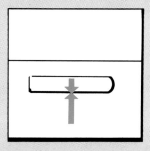 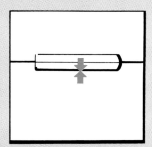

(3) The density of a stone is greater than the density of a swimming float. The force down (its weight) is greater than the push upwards from the water. The net force on the stone is down when you let go and it sinks.

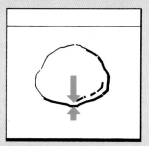

Assessment Task 3d

(1) Ice floats in water because it is less dense than water. The weight of a floating ice cube is equal to the upthrust on it.

(2) A new sponge is very light. It does not soak up much water (until squeezed in water) so, like the swimming float it does not have much weight and does not need to displace much water for forces to balance.

An older, used sponge soaks up water. This adds to its mass (not its volume) so it becomes more dense.

 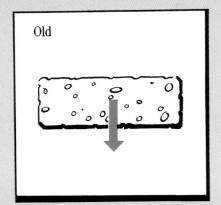

It therefore displaces more water before the forces balance allowing it to float just below the surface.

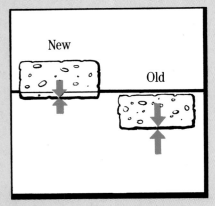

The forces on the sponges balance in each case.

CONCEPTS CHECKLIST

The following concepts are covered in Section 5.

Objects float because of the upthrust by the water.

A push upwards from water makes some objects float.

Adding mass to a 'floater' makes it float lower in the water. Removing mass makes it float higher.

Objects sink when the pull down (gravity) is more than the upthrust.

Your explanation of Assessment Tasks 3a-3d should include the concepts listed above.

ANSWERS

Assessment Task 3a

The candle's mass decreases so it floats higher.

Assessment Task 3b

Item	Volume (cm³)	Mass (g)	Density (g/cm³)	Floats or sinks
Sprout	25	20	0.8	floats
Tomato	40	60	1.5	sinks
Potato	120	130	1.1	sinks
Apple	210	160	0.8	floats
Banana	125	120	0.9	floats
Pear	130	140	1.1	sinks
Orange	200	160	0.8	floats
Carrot	70	80	1.1	sinks
Grape	6	7	1.2	sinks

Assessment Task 3c

(1) The forces down on the float (your push, gravity) balance the push upwards by water. It does not move.

(2) Let go and the push upwards by water is greater than the weight so it moves up to the surface of the water. When it is floating, the push upwards by the water is equal to its weight.

(3) The density of the stone is greater than the density of the water. The net force on the stone is down. It sinks.

Assessment Task 3d

(1) The water pushes back on the ice cube with a force equal to the weight of the ice cube.

(2) The sponge with the greater mass floats lower in the water.

SECTION 6: STRUCTURES

Leaning structures

Task 6a

Identify the balanced forces in these structures.

(1) Lean-to aluminium greenhouse.
(2) Metal clothes airer.
(3) Timber roof rafters.

(1) (2) (3)

  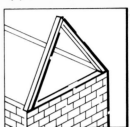

Discussion of Task 6a

In each case the structure pushes on the ground and the ground pushes back.

(1) The greenhouse pushes on the wall and the wall pushes back.

(2) The two halves of the clothes airer push against each other with equal and opposite forces.

(3) The two roof rafters push against each other with equal and opposite forces.

The material from which a structure is made is important. If the greenhouse were made of thin plastic, the force of the wind might make it bend; if the clothes airer were made of card, the weight of clothes would make it bend.

Making bridges

Task 6b

You need two sheets of card, some blocks or books as supports and some small masses. Put folds in one of the sheets and make two bridges as shown.

Test the bridges with the masses to see which is stronger.

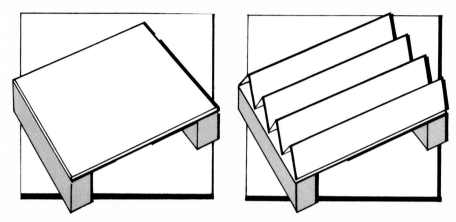

Discussion of Task 6b

The strength can be tested by adding mass to two bridges of equal length until one collapses or by putting the same mass on each bridge and increasing the span until collapse.

Putting folds in the card gives it extra strength.

A shape which is weak in one direction may be stronger in another.

Task 6c

You need two sheets of paper and a piece of card, the supports from Task 6b, glue, a yoghurt pot and some modelling material.

Roll the sheets of paper into cylinders; use them to make the two structures as shown in the illustrations below.

Hang the yoghurt pot with some modelling material in it, from the horizontal cylinder. Add modelling material to the yoghurt pot on the vertical cylinder.

Which arrangement supports the greater load?

Discussion of Task 6c

The vertical cylinder supports a greater load. A cylinder is not a strong shape from which to make a bridge like that in Task 6b.

Task 6d

(1) You need an empty half-eggshell and a piece of card. Arrange them as shown in the illustrations. Using tea, butter, sugar for example find out how much mass it can support. Draw arrows to show the direction of the force on the eggshell.

(2) Make a bridge like the one you tested in Task 6b. Make another bridge, using two sheets, one formed into an arch shape, as shown in the illustration. Test the strength of the two bridges.

Discussion of Task 6d

(1) The weight of the load is not acting directly down; it is being spread over the surface of the shell.

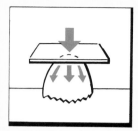

(2) For a fair test you could add a second sheet to the first bridge, so that both bridges are constructed from two sheets of card. The curve of the arch spreads the load on the bridge and makes it stronger than the first bridge.

Task 6e

(1) Cut some straws into 5cm lengths. Join three together to form a triangle and the other four to form a square. (Use pins, pipe cleaners, or screwed-up straws, with glue, for the joints.)

Hold any two corners of the triangle and push gently. What happens?

Do the same with the square. What happens? Keep pushing until your force changes th shape.

Which shape withstands a greater force?

(2) Make three-dimensional shapes so that you have a pyramid and a cube.

Try pushing the corners again and feel which shape is easier to bend.

Which shape seems to have more strength?

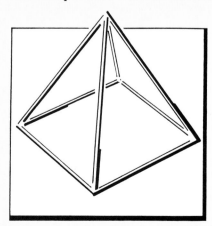
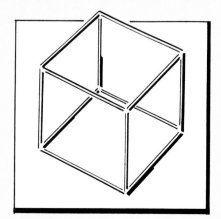

Discussion of Task 6e

(1) Triangles are stronger than squares. Consider trying to change the shape of the triangle by pushing at X.

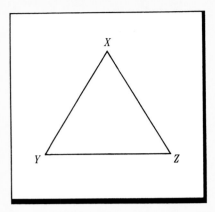

For Y and Z to move apart, the side of the triangle would have to stretch. To change the shape by pushing at Y and Z, the side would have to bend or be squashed. The only other way to change the shape of the triangle is to break the side. The triangle shape can be changed only by stretching, squashing, bending or breaking one of the sides. Imagine the effect of pushing at X to change the shape of a square.

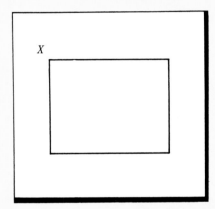

The shape will squash because the angle at the corners is relatively easy to change. The sides are unchanged. The strength is dependent on the way in which the sides are joined together.

(2) Structures which are made of triangles are stronger than those which are made of squares and rectangles.

WHAT THE SCIENTISTS SAY: 12

What does a scientist say about the strength of structures?

The material from which a structure is made can be strengthened by changing its shape. For example folds in plastic help to keep a container rigid. The shapes formed by joining components, for example curves and triangles, contribute to the strength of the structure.

Bridges are shaped so that a load is distributed and therefore does not act in only one place. Instead of the force of the load acting at one point, there are many smaller forces acting across the whole structure. Reaction forces (Newton's Third Law) compensate so there is no overall movement of the bridge, assuming that the components and materials are structurally sound.

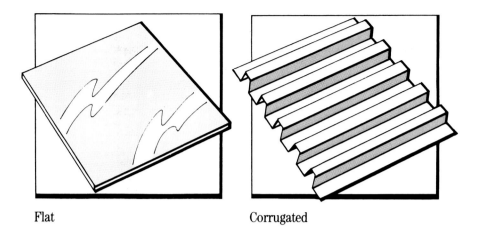

Flat   Corrugated

FURTHER THOUGHTS

Strengthening materials

A structure can be made stronger, not only by changing the material from which it is made but also by changing the shape of the components. A material can be given more strength by changing its shape. For example, a flat sheet of steel will bend in a number of directions when a force is applied to it. Sheets of steel which are used to make the floor of a car have folds put in them. The steel is more difficult to bend when it is corrugated in this way (see the diagram above).

A corrugated sheet of iron, plastic or paper does not bend like a flat sheet. A flat sheet bends in many directions; a corrugated sheet bends easily in one direction only.

Strengthening structures

The shapes which are formed by joining together the components of a structure also contribute to the strength of that structure. Bridge designers often use arches and triangles. These shapes are particularly strong. Strong and stable buildings and structures have balanced forces.

CONCEPT

Shape affects the strength of a structure.

SECTION 7: MORE ON MOVEMENT

Task 7a

In each of the following situations, which one will need the greater force to make it move at a particular velocity? Explain your predictions.

(1) An empty wheelbarrow or a barrow full of rubble.

(2) A child or an adult, each on an office chair with castors.

(3) A small car or a car with passengers and luggage.

(4) A tennis ball or a cricket ball.

Discussion of Task 7a

In each case, the greater mass will need the greater force to accelerate it. So, the full wheelbarrow, the adult on the chair, the loaded car and the cricket ball each need the greater force to start them moving. Such differences were previously considered in Section 2 for a supermarket trolley.

Task 7b

What will happen in cases (1)-(4) if the same force was applied to each? Explain your predictions.

Discussion of Task 7b

In each case, the object with the smaller mass, which needs a smaller force to change its motion, will accelerate at a greater rate than the more massive object.

WHAT THE SCIENTISTS SAY: 13

What does a scientist say about force and mass?

The greater the mass of an object, the more force is required to change its movement. Newton's Second Law of Motion states that: 'A force causes a mass to accelerate in the direction of that force.' A consequence of applying a force to a *stationary* object are that it *starts* to move (it accelerates). Consequences of applying a force to a *moving* object is that it moves faster, it slows down or changes direction.

Task 7c

You need a smooth table top or work surface and a slope, for example a piece of cardboard. You also need a selection of different coins, to include a 10p coin. Slide the 10p coin down the slope so that it hits a 2p coin. Describe what happens. Now use the 10p coin to hit a coin with a different mass – 5p for example. What do you notice? Repeat this, using a 10p coin to hit a number of coins of different mass. Record the differences in movement of the coins which are pushed by the 10p coin and try to explain your observations.

Discussion of Task 7c

Different coins have different masses. They are pushed by the same kind of force each time (if you kept the slope the same and used the 10p coin each time). The bigger the mass, the more force is needed to start the coin moving. The bigger masses tend to travel more slowly after collision. There is a friction force between the coins and the table which stops the bigger coins more quickly. Friction is discussed in Section 8.

WHAT THE SCIENTISTS SAY: 14

How does a scientist define velocity and acceleration?

In physics, direction is important. *Speed* is how fast something is travelling, usually measured in metres per second (but could be centimetres per second or miles per hour). Velocity is a special word which means 'speed in a certain direction' so that, if someone asked you your velocity on the M1 motorway, you should strictly say, for example, '70 miles per hour SOUTH'. When a ball rebounds from a wall, although the *speed* of the ball might not change, its *velocity* does, because the *direction* of movement changes.

Acceleration is defined in terms of velocity. If an object is moving and its velocity is not constant, the rate at which the velocity changes is its acceleration. Acceleration is measured in metres per second (the velocity) per second which can be written as metres/sec/sec or m/s^2.

An acceleration of $4m/s^2$ means that the speed is increasing by 4m/s every second. If the speed started from zero, after one second the speed would be 4m/s, after 2 seconds it would be 8m/s, after 3 seconds it would be 12m/s and so on.

Task 7d

(1) A car is travelling at a constant speed on a motorway. It covers 30km in 50 minutes. What is its speed in m/s?

(2) If the car leaves the motorway and has to go through a town, its average speed decreases because there is a lot of stopping and starting. It covers a further 27km in the next hour before the driver reaches home. What is the average speed, in m/s?

Discussion of Task 7d

(1)   30km = 30,000m; 50 minutes = 3000 seconds; 30,000/3000 = 10m/s.

(2)   27km = 27,000m; 60 minutes = 3600 seconds; 27,000/3600 = 7.5m/s.

Task 7e

At the side of a sports hall is a box with a tennis ball in it. Rolling towards the box is another tennis ball, which has just gone out of play.

Describe the differences between the two balls in terms of forces and movement.

Discussion of Task 7e

The ball in the box has weight due to the force of gravity which pulls it down. It pushes on the box. The reaction force by the box on the ball balances the push and the ball does not move. The same two forces (a pull down and a push up) are acting on the rolling ball. This ball has speed, due to its movement. The speed is decreasing, because of the force of friction (see Section 8) and the ball will stop. While it moves, it also has momentum – although momentum is decreasing because the ball is decelerating.

WHAT THE SCIENTISTS SAY: 15

What does a scientist say about momentum?

If something is moving, you have to push with a force in the opposite direction to the movement to stop it. Two things make it difficult to stop a moving object. First, its *velocity;* the faster an object is moving, the more difficult it is to stop. Second, its *mass:* the greater its mass the more difficult it is to stop. The velocity at which an object is travelling, together with its mass, describe the object's momentum.

The larger the momentum, the more difficult it is to stop an object.

The force applied to an object changes the momentum of the object if it changes its velocity in some way. A force can make a moving object speed up, slow down, change its direction or stop — all of these mean that the object's velocity has changed.

Task 7f

A hockey ball, a tennis ball and a beach ball are dropped in turn into a sandpit. Which one do you think will make the biggest imprint in the sand?

Discussion of Task 7f

The hockey ball is the heaviest; the beach ball is the lightest. If each ball was travelling at the same speed towards the sandpit, the momentum would be greatest for the hockey ball and least for the beach ball.

The sandpit stops each ball moving by applying a force to it. The force applied changes the speed of the ball to zero. The ball with the biggest mass needs the greatest force to stop it, if they are all travelling at the same speed. If two balls have the same mass but are travelling at different speeds, the one travelling faster will need a bigger force to stop it.

The size of the force of the ball on the sand is indicated by the extent of the impact damage in the sand. The hockey ball is likely to make the largest imprint because it has the biggest mass. Another factor affecting the extent of impact damage is the area of sand over which the force is applied. A force spread over a large area will have less effect than if it is spread over a small one. The area over which a force is applied gives a measure of the pressure. This is discussed in Section 9.

Task 7g

Which of the following will need a greater force to stop them moving in a certain time?

(1) Person rolling on a skateboard.

(2) Person on a motorbike.

(3) Person in a car.

Make notes to explain your thinking.

Discussion of Task 7g

The forces required to stop moving objects in the same time are greater for objects with large mass and high speed. Although the total mass in (3) is greater than in (2), if the speed of the motorbike is much greater than the speed of the car there could be more momentum in (2). This is important in road safety; heavy vehicles moving at a high speed need a big force to stop them moving – and such big forces are present in road accidents, e.g. a collision between a car and a lorry. If a lorry has more momentum it requires more force (than the car) to stop it. The force might be strong enough to stop the car, but it would not stop the lorry in the same time, so it keeps going and squashes the car. The knowledge that different shapes have different strengths is applied in the design of cars. This minimises the damage to passengers caused by the forces on cars in accidents.

Task 7h

(1) Try opening a door by pushing at one of the different points indicated each time.

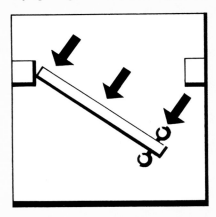

Where was the most force required to move the door? Show the forces involved on a diagram.

(2) Find a tin of drinking chocolate or paint, which has a metal lid. A lever (teaspoon handle or screwdriver, for example) will enable you to remove the lid. Apply force to the lever each time at a different point as indicated in the diagram. Show what was happening on a diagram.

Discussion of Task 7h

(1) The force needed to open the door decreases as the distance from the pivot (the hinge) increases.

(2) The force needed to lift off the lid decreases as the distance from the pivot (the edge of the tin) increases.

WHAT THE SCIENTISTS SAY: 16

What does a scientist say about levers and work?

A lever is a simple machine which uses a pivot. A force is applied to one end of a lever. The further the force is applied from the pivot, the greater the force at the other end of the lever. Similarly, the further the force is applied from the pivot, the less force is required to exert a given force at the other end of the lever. The force applied is less but it has to be applied over a longer distance. In example (1) in Task 7h, the further away from the door hinge you push on the door, the further you have to move, as the door opens. In example (2) your hand pushing on the spoon or screwdriver moves down a long way but the lid lifts up only a short distance.

Work, for the scientist, depends on the force applied and the distance moved. In the case of a lever, at one end a small force moves a long way, doing the same amount of work as the bigger force at the other end which does not move as far.

FURTHER THOUGHTS

Getting started
Forces can make objects start to move from rest. Mass affects how quickly an object can be accelerated.

Keeping going
You read in Section 2 that a push, applied to a stationary object, makes it begin to move and, when the push is removed, the object will continue to move at a constant speed in a straight line, unless another force acts on it. The forces are balanced on an object if it is stationary or if it is moving at a constant velocity.

Stopping things
You know that the greater the mass, the greater the force required to acclerate it to a certain speed, from rest in a certain time. It is equally true that the greater the mass, the greater the force required to stop it moving in a certain time.

Speed, velocity and acceleration
If you put your foot down on the accelerator of a car, your speed (velocity) increases. A high acceleration would mean that your speed was increasing very quickly. The definition of acceleration is 'the rate of change of velocity'. If the velocity changes at a fast rate, you pick up speed quickly and your acceleration is large.

Turning forces
Forces acting on an object can act together to cause the object to turn. The point of turning is the pivot. Any change in movement is about this pivot or fixed point. The greater the distance from the pivot, the less force is needed to make something turn.

CONCEPTS

Forces can change the motion of a moving object.
The greater the mass, the greater the force needed to change an object's movement in a certain time.
Velocity is speed in a particular direction.
Acceleration is the rate of change of velocity.
The momentum of a moving object depends on its mass and velocity.
A turning force has more effect further away from the pivot.

SECTION 8: RESISTANCE TO MOVEMENT

Resistance to movement

Task 8a

Explain the differences in each of the following cases.

(1) Walking on a snow-covered slope in shoes and walking on the same slope in mountain boots.

(2) Running downhill and trying to stop and rollerskating downhill and trying to stop.

Discussion of Task 8a

(1) There is more resistance to movement between the snow and the soles of the boots.

(2) Wheels reduce the resistance to movement between the soles of shoes and the ground.

The resistance is caused by the force of friction.

In earlier examples which involved moving objects, the force of friction was ignored. For example, the force of friction was acting on the car which was pushed (Section 1) and on the rolling marble (Section 2). Once it was moving the car would not continue to roll forever; like the marble, it would slow down and stop.

WHAT THE SCIENTISTS SAY: 17

What does a scientist say about friction?

Friction force is the force which opposes the movement of an object.

Friction will cause heat to be generated: if you rub your hands together, they become slightly warm, as a result of the friction between your palms.

Newton's First Law states that objects continue to move at a fixed velocity unless they are acted on by a force.

Task 8b

Draw the forces which affect the horizontal movement in the following cases:

(1) A car travelling at a constant speed.

(2) A car accelerating.

(3) A moving car whose engine has cut out and is coasting to a stop.

Discussion of Task 8b

(1) The forces on the car are balanced. The forward force is from the engine which turns the wheels which push on the road. The backward force is due to friction.

(2) A net force forward is acting on the car.

(3) The only horizontal force acting on the car is the force of friction. This acts to slow the car down. The arrows on the wheels represent all friction forces.

 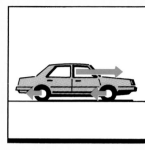 

(1)   (2)   (3)

Although friction forces oppose the motion of the cars in the examples in Task 8b, this does not mean that they are always inconvenient. The car would not move when the wheels turn if there were no friction force between the tyres and the road surface. As you will know if you have ever driven or cycled on an icy surface, when the friction force is reduced, either the wheels turn and the vehicle does not move when you try to accelerate or, when you try to brake, the wheels stop turning and the vehicle keeps moving.

WHAT THE SCIENTISTS SAY: 18

What does a scientist say about air resistance?

Objects moving through air experience the friction force of the air, which acts in the opposite direction to their movement. Air resistance acts against gravity on falling objects and this force increases as the velocity of the object increases.

A falling object speeds up due to the force of gravity. However, as the speed increases, the air resistance increases. If the object is light for its size (not very dense) the force up (air resistance) will soon become equal to the force down (gravity). The object then moves down at a constant velocity because the forces on it are balanced. This velocity is called the terminal velocity (it can go no faster). The air offers a greater resisting force to objects which have a large surface area.

Task 8c

Consider the following falling objects. Draw the forces on each object and explain any differences.

(1) A free-fall sky diver.

(2) A person falling with a parachute.

(3) A paper plate.

(4) A screwed-up paper plate.

Discussion of Task 8c

(1) Gravity is pulling the free-faller down; air resistance pushes up. The faller accelerates until the forces balance – for a person of average mass, the maximum falling velocity is about 200km/hour.

(2) The total weight of the falling body (the person and the parachute) could be greater than that in (1), but the resistance to falling is greatly increased because of the shape of the parachute. The forces on the parachutist balance at a much lower velocity than for the free-faller. The maximum velocity reached before contact with the ground is called the terminal velocity and is only about 6km/hour.

(3) The plate does not have much mass, but has a large surface area. The upward force balances the pull down at a low velocity and the plate falls to the ground. To increase the velocity at which it falls, more mass can be added to the plate. This increases the pull down on the plate, while the push up remains the same.

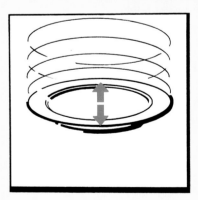

(4) Air resistance is less because the plate presents a smaller area to the air as it falls. The pull down is the same. The forces balance at a greater speed than in (3).

Discussion of Task 8c continued

Why does anything ever move?

If the forces on an object balance, the movement of the object does not change. The force of one object on another is matched by an equal and opposite reaction force.

Consider these three situations.

(1) The book resting on the table.

(2) A toy being pulled.

(3) A ball falling.

(1) There are four forces acting in this situation.

  (i)   The Earth pulls the book downward (the force of gravity on the book).
  (ii) The book pulls the Earth upward.
  (iii) The book pushes the table downward.
  (iv) The table pushes the book upward.

As far as Newton's Third Law is concerned, these go in pairs: (i) and (ii) go together (action and reaction) and (iii) and (iv) go together (action and reaction). However, as far as the book is concerned, there are two forces *on it*. They are (i) and (iv) and these are the two forces which balance out and keep the book stationary.

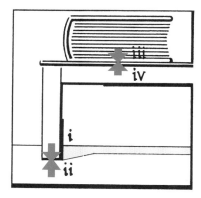

(2) The action/reaction pair of forces is at the point where the string attaches to the toy. The string pulls on the toy and the surface of the toy pulls back (the converse of the book on the table). The net force *on the toy* is in the direction of the pull.

(3) For falling objects the action/reaction pair of forces is described by Newton's Law of Gravity. The Earth pulls the ball towards it and the ball pulls the Earth back with the same force. Air resistance is small: it pushes up on the surface of the ball. The net force *on the ball* is down and it accelerates towards the ground. The reason that the Earth does not move but the ball does is that the mass of the Earth is much greater than that of the ball. A greater mass requires a greater force to start it moving.

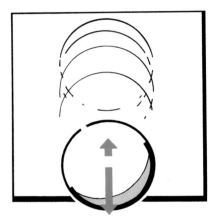

FURTHER THOUGHTS

Keeping things moving along the ground
If an object is moving at a constant velocity, there is no net force acting on it.

Falling things
Earlier in the book you considered a ball, a conker and a fir cone falling. There is a friction force, in each case, which opposes the movement of the object. This is the force of air resistance.
Gravity pulls a falling object down and changes its movement – it speeds up. The resisting force by the air pushes up on the object and changes as the speed of the object changes. The strength of air resistance also depends on the size and shape of the object.

CONCEPTS

Friction forces oppose motion.
Air resistance is a friction force.

SECTION 9: PRESSURE

A force spread over a big area is different from the same force acting at a point (see discussion on snow shoes in Section 1).

Task 9a

Sketch the following situations and draw the force acting in each. Explain the difference in the effect of that force when it is spread over a large area.

(1) Cutting modelling material. If instead of pushing down with a coin on a lump of modelling material, you used a knife, and pushed with the same force, the knife would go further into the modelling material.

(2) On the beach, walking on sand in bare feet does not hurt; walking on pebbles and small stones does.

(3) When climbing a ladder the rungs of a ladder can hurt your feet if they are round rather than flat steps, particularly if you are wearing soft-soled shoes.

(4) The forces on a mattress. Consider the difference between lying on a mattress and standing on it.

(5) Shoes – the same person can make a different impression on a cushion floor, depending on the area of the heel of their shoe. Stiletto heels make a deeper indentation than flat heels.

Discussion of Task 9a

(1) The pushing force needed to make an imprint from the coin acts on the modelling material over an area the size of the coin. The same force on the knife acts over a much smaller area (the blade edge) and the knife moves further into the modelling material.

 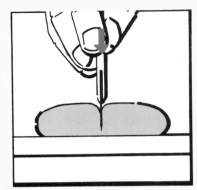

(2) The reaction force on the feet is spread over the whole of the sole, on the sand. This is the force that feet are used to experiencing, walking on flat ground. The reaction force is the same (because the body weight is the same) from the pebbles but it is acting on a number of much smaller areas, corresponding to the contact points of the pebbles. The total contact area is reduced.

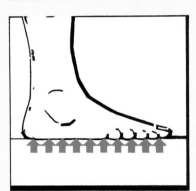 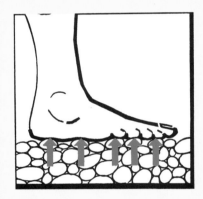

(3) This is similar to the experience on the beach. The reaction force is the same, whatever ladder is climbed. The flat step provides a bigger area of contact for the foot and the force is spread out. Wearing stiff-soled shoes helps in the same way to spread the reaction force.

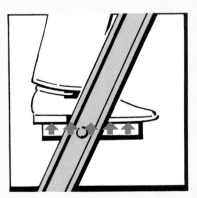 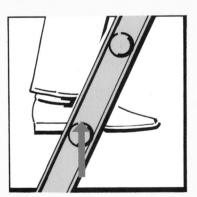

(4) The force on the mattress is the same. When the force acts through feet, it is pushing on the mattress over a small area.

 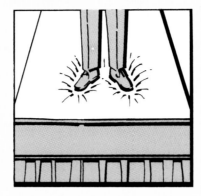

(5) A woman might exert a weight of 500N through the heels of her shoes. If she wears broad-heeled shoes with a total area of 20cm², she exerts a pressure of $500/20N/cm^2 = 25N/cm^2$. If she wears stiletto-heeled shoes with a total area of 2.5cm², she would exert a pressure through the heel of $500/2.5N/cm^2 = 200N/cm^2$.

Discussion of Task 9a continued

WHAT THE SCIENTISTS SAY: 19

What does a scientist say about pressure?

Pressure is not the same as force. The pressure on an object is a measure of the force acting on a square centimetre or square metre of the object. Pressure is measured in Newtons per square centimetre (N/cm²) or Newtons per square metre (N/m²).

FURTHER THOUGHTS

Reducing pressure
A force spread over a big area can have a different effect from the same force acting at a point, e.g. wearing snow shoes spreads your force (weight) over a larger area thereby reducing the force at any point. The snow shoes thus reduce your pressure on the snow and you don't sink in as far.

CONCEPT

Pressure is a measure of how much force is acting on a particular area of an object.

SELF-ASSESSMENT: PART 4

Before you work through this section, make sure that you have completed Sections 6, 7, 8 and 9. Work on previous sections will also be assessed.

The supermarket offers many illustrations of forces in everyday life. All of the following situations could be experienced whilst shopping.

Assessment Task 4a

An empty trolley rolls slowly and harmlessly into a display. Why does it do no damage to the display?

Assessment Task 4b

A heavily laden trolley is difficult to turn at the end of an aisle. Why is this?

Assessment Task 4c

A heavily laden trolley bumps into a display and almost knocks it over. Why was the impact of this trolley more significant that in Task 4a above?

Assessment Task 4d

A full trolley is pulled-up quickly. Loose items tumble from the top. Why is the trolley difficult to stop and why do the items fall in front of the trolley?

Assessment Task 4e

A heavily laden trolley hits another heavily laden trolley and an empty trolley standing next to it. The second laden trolley hardly moves but the empty trolley shoots off and stops abruptly when it hits some bags of potatoes.

Explain what is happening when the trolleys collide, in terms of mass, speed and force. What is happening in terms of forces when the empty trolley is stopped by the potatoes?

Assessment Task 4f

Tomatoes at the bottom of a full trolley are squashed and a packet of sugar bursts.

What forces are involved to squash the tomatoes?

Draw a diagram to explain the difference, in terms of forces, between the sugar contained in a whole bag and what happens to the sugar when the bag bursts.

Assessment Task 4g

Heavy carrier bags are sometimes painful to carry, the same load in a box is less painful.

Why do the bags hurt your hands more?

Assessment Task 4h

A full trolley is wheeled across the car park and turned around to unload it.

What are the forces on the trolley, in the car park?

Assessment Task 4i

A supermarket trolley will not collapse under heavy load.

How does the structure of a supermarket trolley give it strength?

Assessment Task 4j

A heavy trolley is released at the top of a slope. It gets faster and faster.

Explain the effect of the forces on the trolley.

COMMENTARY

Assessment Task 4a

An object continues to move at the same speed and in a straight line unless acted on by a force. The force by the trolley on the display caused an equal and opposite force on the trolley, the trolley decelerated (slowed down – negative acceleration) and stopped.

This incident can be explained in terms of momentum:

momentum = mass × velocity.

The trolley had a small mass and was not moving fast so momentum was small. The force required to stop an object depends on its momentum and the time taken to stop it. Had the trolley been moving more quickly then its momentum would have been greater and more damage would have occurred.

Assessment Task 4b

An object (such as the trolley) will continue in a straight line at the same speed unless acted on by a force. It follows that a force was required to cause the trolley to change direction at the end of the aisle. Changing its direction of movement changes the velocity, so the momentum ($m \times v$) was changed. The size of force depends on how heavy the trolley was, how fast it was moving, and how quickly the trolley changed direction.

Assessment Task 4c

The heavier mass and increased velocity means that more force was needed to change the movement of the trolley in a certain time, in this case to stop it. The trolley was full, therefore the force needed to stop it in the same time was considerably more than in Assessment Task 4a. Stopping it changes its velocity so the momentum changes.

Assessment Task 4d

The force required to stop the trolley was again considerable because of the large mass of the shopping and its large momentum.

The items on the top of the shopping were travelling at the same speed as the rest of the shopping when the trolley was stopped. However, they were not fixed on the trolley and the friction force between them and the rest of the shopping was not enough to stop their movement. They continued on in a straight line but fell to the floor due to the force of gravity.

Direction of movement

Assessment Task 4e

Assume that the uncontrolled trolley hit both trolleys with the same force for the same time. The uncontrolled trolley had more mass than the empty trolley so the empty one picked up speed quicker and travelled further. The empty trolley hit the bags of potatoes and slowed down to stop (decelerated). This was due to the force on the trolley by the bags of potatoes. The situation is similar to the trolley hitting the display. The second laden trolley hardly moves because the same force can only give such a large mass a small acceleration.

Assessment Task 4f

Consider the forces on a squashed tomato. The weight of shopping pushed down on the tomato which in turn pushed down on the trolley. The trolley pushed back on the tomato causing it to squash. The force of gravity pulls the sugar downwards. The sugar pushes on the paper bag which, in turn, pushes on the trolley cage. The trolley cage pushes up on the paper bags with a force which is equal and opposite. The bag is strong enough to spread the force over the sugar and push it up. There is no net force on the sugar. When the bag is punctured the force of gravity pulls the sugar down. There is no force up from the bag or the trolley and sugar accelerates to the floor.

Assessment Task 4g

If the mass of shopping in the box and in the bags is the same, the push down on your hand is the same. This force on your hand is spread, by the box, over a bigger area. The pressure by the bags on your fingers is greater and the bag handles can feel as though they are 'cutting' into your fingers.

Assessment Task 4h

There was the force of gravity giving the trolley its weight, and the push up on the wheels from the road.

The trolley was pushed to keep it moving and the friction force between the road and the wheels opposed the movement. When the push and the friction force were equal the speed of the trolley was constant.

Assessment Task 4i

The structure of the supermarket trolley uses a triangular shape to brace the basket and give it the strength to support heavy loads.

Assessment Task 4j

The trolley accelerated because the force of gravity exceeded the friction force resisting movement; the trolley moved faster and faster.

CONCEPTS CHECKLIST

The following concepts are from all the sections.

Forces can change the motion of a moving object.
The greater the mass, the greater the force needed to change an object's movement.
The greater the speed, the greater force needed to change an object's movement.
Velocity is speed in a particular direction.
Acceleration is the rate of change of velocity.
The momentum of a moving object depends on its mass and velocity.
Friction forces oppose motion.
A turning force has more effect further away from the pivot.
Shape affects the strength of a structure.
Pressure is a measure of how much force is acting on a particular area of an object.

Your explanation of Assessment Tasks 4a-4j should include the concepts listed above.

ANSWERS

Assessment Task 4a

A trolley pushed the display and the display pushed back.
Forces act in pairs.
The force by the display on the trolley changed the movement of the trolley.
A small mass requires a small force to stop it in a certain time.
A slow speed requires a small force to stop it in a certain time.
The momentum of the trolley depends on its mass and its velocity.

Assessment Task 4b

A force can change the movement of the trolley.
A force is needed to change the trolley's direction.
The velocity of the trolley changes
The force needed depends on the mass of the trolley and the time taken to change direction.
The force needed depends on the speed of the
trolley and the time taken to change direction.
The momentum of the trolley depends on its mass and velocity.

Assessment Task 4c

Increased mass means more force is needed to stop the trolley in a certain time.
Increased velocity means more force is needed to stop the trolley in a certain time.
A force is needed to slow down the moving trolley.

Assessment Task 4d

A force is needed to stop the trolley.
The pull was in the opposite direction to the movement of the trolley, in order to stop it.
It was a large force because the trolley has a large mass and is fast moving and has stopped in a short distance.
The friction force on the loose items was not enough to stop them moving.
Gravity pulled the loose items to the ground.

Assessment Task 4e

The uncontrolled trolley decelerated and stopped.
To stop the trolley a force must act on it.
The mass and velocity of the rogue trolley and the time taken to stop it determines the force needed to stop it.
The empty trolley has a smaller mass than the second laden trolley and so moves off quicker when hit with the same force.
The empty trolley has a small mass so the force needed to stop it moving is small (compared with the full trolley).

Assessment Task 4f

The force of the push down and the force up from the trolley result in the tomatoes being squashed.
The force down of the weight of the sugar is equal and opposite to the force exerted by the bag.
When the bag bursts there is no force up on the sugar, the only force is the weight of the sugar.

Assessment Task 4g

A force spread over a smaller area exerts a greater pressure.

Assessment Task 4h

The trolley has weight which pushes on the ground and the ground pushes up on the trolley.
A force is required to start the trolley moving.
The ground applied a friction force which opposed the motion of the trolley.
The force required to change the trolley's movement in a certain time depends on the mass of the trolley, its velocity and the friction forces.
To turn the trolley requires a force.

Assessment Task 4i

The construction of the trolley uses triangles which are difficult to squash.

Assessment Task 4j

The force needed to cause the trolley to move is determined by its mass.
The velocity of the trolley was not constant, it accelerated.
The force of gravity causes the moving trolley to speed up; it was a greater force than the friction forces.

GLOSSARY

Acceleration (a) The rate of change of *velocity* is called acceleration. A body which is accelerating may be changing its *speed* or its direction of movement. Acceleration due to gravity on Earth is $9.8m/s^2$, i.e. 9.8 metres per second, every second.

Air resistance Air resistance is the friction force on bodies moving through air. The size of the force of air resistance on a body depends on its shape and speed.

Archimedes' Principle When a body is immersed in a fluid the upthrust force on the object is equal to the weight of fluid displaced.

Density Density is the property of a body determined by the relationship between its mass and volume. Objects which have a high density are *heavy for their size*. Objects with a low density are *light for their size*.

$$Density = \frac{mass}{volume}.$$

For example – expanded polystyrene has a density of $0.1g/cm^3$, water has a density of $1.00g/cm^3$ and gold has a density of $19.3g/cm^3$, i.e. $1cm^3$ of polystyrene has a mass of 0.1g

$$\frac{0.1}{1} = 0.1g/cm^3;$$

$1cm^3$ of water has a mass of 1g

$$\frac{1}{1} = 1g/cm^3;$$

$1cm^3$ of gold has a mass of 19.3g

$$\frac{19.3}{1} = 19.3g/cm^3.$$

Energy Energy is 'what makes things happen', the capacity for activity, the ability to do work.

Floating An object will float in water (or any other fluid) if the weight of the fluid which it displaces is equal to its own weight. In other words, the force up and the force down on the body are equal.

Force (F) A force is a push or a pull. Forces can act to *change the movement or change the shape of* objects they act on. Forces are measured in Newtons (N).

Free-fall An object which is falling to Earth under the effects of gravitational force is said to be 'in free-fall'. Freely falling objects accelerate towards the Earth at a rate of $9.8m/s^2$. This rate applies to all compact objects falling due to the Earth's gravitational pull.

Friction force The force acting to oppose the motion of one body in relation to another.

Gravitational force The pull on a body due to the Earth's gravity which gives the body its weight. An object with a mass of 1kg has a force on Earth of 10N acting on it due to gravity.

Inertia   A property of a body due to its mass. It is an indication of how hard it is to start and stop the body moving. The more massive the body the more difficult it will be to get it to begin to move or to stop.

Kilogram (kg)   The standard unit of mass is the kilogram (kg). A *mass* of *1kg* on Earth will have a *weight* of 10N due to the Earth's gravitational force.

Lever   A lever is a simple machine in which force is applied over a distance from a pivot. The longer the lever, the less force is needed to move the load on the opposite side of the pivot.

Machines   In general terms, any machine is something which allows us to do a job or work using less force than we would otherwise need. Levers, pulleys, ramps and gears are all simple machines.

Mass (m)   The amount of matter or 'stuff' in a body is the mass (m). Mass is a property of a body, measured in kilograms (kg). It should not be confused with *weight* which is a force.

Momentum   This is an indication of how much force is needed to stop a moving body. Momentum depends on the mass of a body and how fast it is moving.

Momentum = mass $\times$ velocity ($m \times v$).

For example, a heavy lorry moving slowly has less momentum than the same lorry moving quickly; a heavy lorry has more momentum than a light lorry moving at the same velocity.

Newton (N)   The SI unit of force (and therefore weight) is the Newton (N). One Newton is that force which, when acting on a mass of 1kg, causes it to accelerate at the rate of $1m/s^2$.

Newton's Laws of Motion

First law –   A body will remain in a state of rest, or uniform motion in a straight line, unless acted on by a force.

Second law –   A force acting on a body causes it to accelerate in the direction of the force. The size of the acceleration depends on the size of the force and the mass of the body: $F = m \times a$.

Third law –   To every action by a body A on B, there is an equal reaction in the opposite direction by B on A.

Newton meter   This is a spring balance which is calibrated in Newtons (not kilograms) used to measure force (and therefore weight).

Power   Power is the *rate* at which something can do work:

$$Power = \frac{work\ done}{time\ taken}$$

Power is measured in Joules per second (J/s) or Watts (W).

Pressure   The relationship between a force and the area on which it acts is the pressure:

$$\text{Pressure} = \frac{\text{force}}{\text{area}}$$

Pressure is measured in Newtons per square metre (N/m^2) or Newtons per square centimetre (N/cm^2). Pressure can be reduced if the area on which it acts is increased.

Speed   The distance travelled by an object in a given time is its speed.

$$\text{Speed} = \frac{\text{distance moved}}{\text{time taken}}$$

Stability   The stability of an object gives an indication of how easy, or difficult, it is to tip the object over. Objects with most of their weight at their base, that is with a low centre of gravity, will be more stable than those with their weight centred towards the top.

Velocity (v)   The velocity of an object is the speed *in a given direction*. Objects which are moving are doing so at a certain rate and in a certain direction:

$$\text{Velocity} = \frac{\text{distance moved}}{\text{time taken}}$$

Volume   The amount of space which a body takes up is the volume. Volume is measured in cubic centimetres (cm^3).

Weight   The downward force acting on a body due to the effect of gravitational force is weight. Gravitational forces are dependent on the masses of the bodies, so the weight of a body on the Earth is different from its weight on the Moon. Weight is measured in Newtons (N).

Work   Work is done when a force makes something move. The amount of work done depends on the size of the force and the distance moved in the direction of the force.

Work done = force $\times$ distance.

RESOURCES

Section 3

Task 3a   A potato and a fir cone of similar size

Task 3c   Kitchen weighing scales, ball of modelling material, large bag of cotton wool

Section 4

Task 4d   An unopened pack of butter, a paper clip, an elastic band, balance scales with two pans, masses, string and scissors

Task 4f   A set of bathroom scales, an elastic band and a ruler, or a Newton meter

Section 5

Task 5a   A large empty plastic bottle (e.g. fabric conditioner or shampoo)

Task 5b   A collection of objects (some of which do not float), string, a paper clip, an elastic band and a ruler.

Task 5c   Tea bag, mug, kettle, bowl of water, modelling material, paper clips

Task 5e   A collection of objects, kitchen scales, measuring jug

Task 5f   Modelling material, a table tennis ball, measuring jug, kitchen scales

Task 5g $5cm^3$ teaspoon, salt, sugar, measuring jug

Section 6

Task 6b   Two sheets of card, some blocks or books, small masses

Task 6c   Two sheets of paper, one sheet of card, glue, a yoghurt pot, modelling material

Task 6d   An empty half eggshell, a piece of card, packs of butter, tea and sugar. Blocks or books, two sheets of card

Task 6e   Modelling straws, pins, glue

Section 7

Task 7c   A selection of coins, a piece of cardboard, a smooth work surface

Task 7h   A teaspoon or screwdriver, a tin with a metal lid, e.g. drinking chocolate